AIR POWER IN WAR

Air Power in War

ARTHUR WILLIAM TEDDER

INTRODUCTION BY VINCENT ORANGE

THE UNIVERSITY OF ALABAMA PRESS
Tuscaloosa, Alabama

The University of Alabama Press
Tuscaloosa, Alabama 35487-0380
Manufactured in the United States of America

The introduction by Vincent Orange is used with the permission of the author.
"Air, Land and Sea Warfare" is reproduced with the permission of *Flight International*, January 17, 1946, p. 68.

Printing history:
Hodder and Stoughton hardcover edition / 1947
The University of Alabama Press paperback edition / 2010

∞

Library of Congress Cataloging-in-Publication Data

Tedder, Arthur William Tedder, Baron, 1890–1967.
  Air power in war / Arthur William Tedder ; introduction by Vincent Orange.
     p. cm.
  Originally published: London : Hodder and Stoughton, 1947.
With new introd.
    Includes bibliographical references.
    ISBN 978-0-8173-5625-5 (pbk. : alk. paper) — ISBN 978-0-8173-8534-7 (electronic) 1. World War, 1939–1945—Aerial operations. I. Title.
    D785.T4 2010
    940.54'4—dc22
                                                      2010006477

Cover image: (left to right) British Field Marshal Bernard L. Montgomery, American General and future president, Dwight Eisenhower, and Air Marshal Sir Arthur Tedder posing during a Supreme Command Tour, winter of 1944/5. Photo by Frank Scherschel for Time Life Pictures. Courtesy of Getty Images.

CONTENTS

LIST OF DIAGRAMS

LIFE AND CAREER OF
ARTHUR WILLIAM TEDDER

Arthur William Tedder, 1st Baron Tedder, G.C.B. (1890–1967), was born at Glenguin (now Glengoyne), a distillery about twenty miles north of Glasgow on July 11, 1890. He was the youngest of three children to Arthur John Tedder, an excise and revenue official, and Emily Charlotte Bryson Tedder.

Frequent moves caused by his father's excise duties ensured a varied upbringing for Tedder: the family lived in Lerwick in the Shetlands and Elgin, near the Moray coast of Scotland. From 1902–09 he attended the Whitgift School, Croydon, south London. He excelled in military exercises with the Officers' Training Corps (O.T.C.), becoming a crack shot. A natural navigator, he learned to read the stars easily.

Tedder's talents then flourished at Magdalene College, Cambridge, from 1909–13; he was encouraged by his tutors to study German at an institute in Berlin during the summer, then return to school to prepare for a diplomatic career.

Tedder abandoned his diplomatic prospects in 1913, and an academic career did not appeal either. He accepted a position as a Colonial Office cadet in Fiji and left England in February 1914. He was soon unhappy with his post and prospects; however, the outbreak of war cleared his path. Eager to join the regular army, he resigned and returned to England in December.

Commissioned as a second lieutenant in the Dorsetshire regiment in January 1915, Tedder joined the 3rd Reserve Battalion at Wyke Regis, near Weymouth. A serious knee injury in February held him in Wyke until July, then at a base camp in Calais until October. There he sought a transfer to the Royal Flying Corps (R.F.C.). In January 1916 when he was fully mobile again, the R.F.C. accepted Tedder, and his progress was astonishing. Promoted to captain in March, he was taught to fly in April, and joined the 25th Squadron—a unit equipped with the FE2b, a two-seater with its engine placed behind the crew—on the western front in June. On June 21 he wrote to his wife that an anti-aircraft gun "put a shrapnel bullet through the nacelle of my aircraft, in one side and out the other, cutting one of the petrol pipes and passing down between my legs. Petrol came pouring out in a continuous stream over my right foot." Fortunately, flames did not appear and a career that had barely begun did not end. Appointed flight commander in August, Tedder was promoted to major in command of 70 Squadron for six months from January 1917. His new squadron flew the Sopwith 1½ Strutter, the RFCR.F.C.'s first aircraft with a machinegun firing through the propeller arc and the observer seated *behind* the pilot.

Although he was an excellent navigator and a competent pilot with the 25 Squadron, flying in combat as well as carrying out reconnaissance, photography, escort, and bombing tasks, Tedder's main strength was on the ground with 70 Squadron when his duties prevented him from flying regularly. Older than most pilots and more thoroughly educated, he was able to shift paper swiftly and thereby pacify higher command. He also had the calm temperament and good humor needed to see men through the many periods of heavy casualties. Hugh Trenchard, head of the R.F.C. in France, and a man who made or marred numerous careers, noticed him favorably; so too did Wilfrid Freeman, an officer who later helped Tedder into high command and sustained him there.

In July 1917 at Shawbury in Shropshire, Tedder had his first taste of the tasks in which he later specialized: large-scale training in air fighting, gunnery, and artillery observation. In May 1918 he was sent to Cairo to organize similar training, but his ship was torpedoed upon leaving Marseilles. He was rescued by a Japanese destroyer—a distinction, he claimed, unmatched by any other senior British officer. Promoted to lieutenant colonel in July 1918, he adroitly handled discontent over demobilization problems at the end of the war. He returned to England in March 1919, rejected an offer to resume his Colonial Office career in April, was granted a permanent commission as a squadron leader in August, and took command of the 207 Squadron at Bircham Newton, Norfolk, in February 1920.

By September 1922 when the Chanak crisis (a Turkish challenge to British control of the Dardanelles) threatened to escalate into war, Tedder had so impressed Trenchard that his was one of three squadrons sent from England to Constantinople in support of a strong naval and military force. Tedder remained there for nine hard months, helping to ensure that the threat remained dormant. During that time he revived the reputation he had won on the western front. It was founded on sensible, consistent discipline; a practical concern to improve living conditions; a readiness to share information with all ranks; and plenty of realistic training. Throughout a sensitive period, he avoided incidents, not only with Turks, Greeks, or Russians, but also with senior British naval or army officers or French allies. His excellent performance confirmed Trenchard's good opinion, and in July 1923 he was selected for the Royal Naval Staff College course at Greenwich the following October. The R.A.F.'s own college had opened only the previous year, and the infant service was desperately short on staff-trained officers.

At Greenwich, Tedder wrote thoughtful essays on anti-shipping bombs, warplane design, and cloud-flying problems; in January 1924 he was promoted to wing commander.

From Greenwich, he took command in September of a flying training station at Digby, Lincolnshire. His practical ideas to improve flying standards impressed Freeman, now commandant of the Central Flying School. So did his efforts to make Digby a place where officers and men were content as well as busy: he instructed his men to plant bushes and flowers, clean and paint buildings, and he encouraging sports and hobbies. All of this helped to create a well-disciplined family atmosphere, which he tried to do wherever he sered.

In January 1927 his reward was a senior Air Ministry appointment: deputy director of training. An even higher mark of favor came in January 1928 when he was sent to study for one year at the Imperial Defence College, near Buckingham Palace. At the college, promising officers from all three services and civil servants considered matters of high policy, advised by government ministers and senior politicians. Tedder was then appointed a member of the directing staff at the R.A.F. Staff College, Andover, in 1929–30, and in 1931 on his promotion to group captain was named deputy commandant. He developed a talent for cogent argument, on paper or across a table, and wrote three studies of the Gallipoli campaign, focusing particularly on interservice cooperation when attempting a landing upon a hostile shore. These were problems that would deeply concern him a decade later.

After commanding an air armament school at Eastchurch, Essex, in 1932–34, Tedder returned to the Air Ministry in April 1934 as director of training and was promoted to air commodore in July. Until September 1936 he was responsible for flying, armament, and navigation training, with an interest in the effective use of weapons; and he kept in touch with designers, manufacturers, and government departments. These were years of reorganization and expansion to face the prospect of another war, and on his initiative, civilian schools took over elementary flying training, leaving service schools free to concentrate on advanced training and to provide operational squadrons with better-prepared crews.

Tedder was sent to Singapore in October 1936 as head of a command stretching from Burma to Hong Kong and on to Borneo. Promoted to air vice-marshal in July 1937, he reformed the air staff organization, visited every unit, improved relations with other services, sought sites for new airfields, and helped to devise and conduct realistic triservice exercises to counter a possible Japanese attack.

In July 1938 Freeman, now air member for research and development, had Tedder brought back to England to take an Air Ministry appointment as director-general of research and development. Until December 1940 he and Freeman worked with managing directors, chief designers, and senior trade union officials from aircraft manufacturers and their suppliers to provide Britain with aircraft, weapons, and equipment capable of resisting the Luftwaffe and carrying the war to Germany.

The task was complicated by a revolution in the design, construction, equipment, and production of aircraft. It was a revolution so profound that several promising ventures failed for technical reasons, such as the Westland Whirlwind, a twin-engine cannon-armed fighter that was a favorite of Tedder's, while others, notably Whittle's jet engine, were not pushed energetically, although Tedder himself was among Whittle's supporters.

A complication arose in May 1940 when the entire aircraft enterprise was detached from the Air Ministry and made part of a new Ministry of Aircraft Production under the control of Lord Beaverbrook. In Tedder's opinion, Beaverbrook's management was flawed, so he sought to escape. Freeman, who had returned to the Air Ministry as vice-chief of the air staff, supported a request in November 1940 from Arthur

Longmore, head of Middle East command in Cairo, that Tedder be appointed his deputy. Prime Minister Churchill, advised by Beaverbrook, preferred another officer who unfortunately fell into Italian hands on the way to Cairo, and Churchill then saw Tedder promoted to air marshal. Tedder arrived in Cairo in December and succeeded Longmore in command in May 1941. He quickly impressed Charles Portal, chief of the air staff from October 1940, with his abilities, and at Portal's request Tedder sent regular and brutally frank reports on the Mediterranean scene. By October 1941 he had earned the confidence of Claude Auchinleck, the army commander, whose support, allied to that of Portal and Freeman, prevented Churchill from sacking him over a dispute about air strength on the eve of Operation Crusader in November 1941.

In Cairo, Tedder assembled an outstanding team, headed by Peter Drummond (his deputy) and Grahame Dawson (in charge of repair and maintenance) with Arthur Coningham (field commander), assisted by Thomas Elmhirst (responsible for administration and supply). In March 1943 he recruited as his chief scientific adviser Solly Zuckerman, a biologist who transformed himself after 1939 into an expert on the effects of bombing. Tedder frequently left his office—as in his squadron commander days—to talk to all ranks, and as later described by the *Times* became "the most unstuffy of great commanders, who could be found sitting cross-legged, jacketless, pipe smouldering, answering questions on a desert airstrip." He was promoted to air chief marshal in July 1942.

Success in the desert war, achieved by November 1942, commended Tedder to Dwight D. Eisenhower, an American general newly arrived in northwest Africa as supreme allied commander, and to Carl A. Spaatz, head of American air forces there. They formed a triumvirate, which did much to balance increasingly tense relations with Bernard Montgomery, the exceptional but single-minded British field commander. As head of Mediterranean air command beginning in February 1943, Tedder recast Anglo-American air power into an effective force, ending early setbacks and helping to bring about complete victory in Tunisia by May 1943, followed by the conquest of Sicily in August and the invasion of Italy in September.

In December 1943 Tedder was appointed Eisenhower's deputy for Operation Overlord, launched in June 1944 to liberate Europe. Advised by Zuckerman, Tedder persuaded Eisenhower to require a prolonged, systematic attack on enemy marshalling yards that controlled rail systems serving the invasion area in order to prevent the Germans from moving reinforcements and heavy weapons quickly. Churchill, fearing the political consequences of French and Belgian civilian casualties, urged President Roosevelt to cancel the plan, but Roosevelt supported Eisenhower. About seven thousand civilians did die, a much number than those killed by ground fighting after D-day.

From August 1944 after the breakout from Normandy, this plan intended the paralysis of Germany's industry, commerce, and agriculture by inhibiting all movement. Raw materials are useless unless they are sent to factories, turned into weapons or something as vital, and then delivered where they are needed; harvested crops are of little value unless they can be moved from where they are grown to where they are eaten; and synthetic oil, essential to German military operations, could not be produced without coal, which also must be transported from the mine to a refinery.

Arthur Harris, commanding the British night bomber force, preferred to continue destruction of German cities, and General Carl Spaatz, commanding American day bombers, wanted to focus on aircraft factories, oil targets, and their defending fighters. Tedder gradually won support for his plan from both men as well as cooperation from the immense allied tactical air forces. It was less than he thought ideal, but perhaps as much as he could obtain without fracturing the façade of Anglo-American unity, which he and Eisenhower were determined to maintain. When hostilities ceased, Tedder went as Eisenhower's representative to Berlin, where he and Russian commander Marshal Zhukov shared the honor and satisfaction of receiving the formal German surrender on May 9.

Two principles had guided Tedder's years of command throughout the Mediterranean and northwest European campaigns. First, the need for close relations with the United States at whatever cost to British influence over grand strategy, since British industry could not provide sufficient weapons (ground or air) to avoid defeat, let alone achieve victory. American supplies were already essential for the desert war in 1941, and American manpower would become so for the Overlord campaign. Second, the need for centralized control of air power; Tedder insisted on this, overcoming strong opposition from naval and army commanders. Air superiority, he argued, must be sought before close support at sea or on land could be implemented. Also, he must be the judge, advised by his field commanders, of where and when that support could best be offered.

Tedder achieved five-star rank (marshal of the Royal Air Force) in September 1945 and succeeded Portal as chief of the air staff on January 1, 1946. In June he was appointed chairman of the chiefs of staff committee, working with Montgomery (army) and John Cunningham (navy). Montgomery detested all committees and despised his colleagues, who returned the sentiment with interest. The work got done—often by deputies—but harmony was not restored until November 1948, when Prime Minister Attlee, found Montgomery another important position.

In August 1947 Tedder organized exercise Thunderbolt, a four-day study of the strategic air offensive between 1943 and 1945. Those officers still serving who had helped to direct that offensive were required to revive their memories and even to take part in scripted reconstructions of significant episodes. They were helped by secret documents, especially reports by the British bombing survey unit, prepared under Zuckerman's direction. Unsurprisingly, the results supported Tedder's campaign against German rail assets, and four lectures that Tedder had delivered at Cambridge earlier that year were published in 1948 as *Air Power in War*.

Two equally elaborate exercises followed: Pandora (on scientific and technical aides to air war) in May 1948, and Ariel (on manpower problems) in April 1949.

Tedder's air force had responsibilities stretching from Germany to Hong Kong via the Middle East, but following massive demobilization in 1945–46, there were too few skilled long-service personnel to cope with them properly. Although the day of piston-engine warplanes was clearly ending, funds were unavailable, in peacetime, for the rapid development of jet successors. By 1948 many demands exacerbated these problems: the Berlin airlift, unrest in Malaya, and especially concern over the Middle East and the need to safeguard oil supplies, protect sea links with the Far East, and provide for effective defense in the event of Soviet aggression.

Tedder supervised reforms in organization, recruitment drives, and the restoration in 1948 of a British radar-based defense system, which was linked to an enlarged Fighter Command. Above all he encouraged the closest relations with American airmen, quietly preparing, from 1946 onward, bases in England for their strategic bombers and attempting to standardize equipment and training. But he also supported the decision that Britain must have its own nuclear weapons, and planning began in 1948 for a British jet bomber force capable of carrying them.

Tedder was succeeded on January 1, 1950, by John Slessor, an outstanding officer widely regarded as the obvious heir. On most service issues they agreed, but in method and temperament they differed markedly. As early as 1947, Tedder had tried, but failed, to remove Slessor from contention; he failed again in 1949. Ralph Cochrane was his choice, but Slessor's superior merits (strongly supported behind closed doors by Trenchard, Portal, and Freeman) earned him the position. Slessor immediately offered Cochrane the position of vice-chief, which he accepted.

Tedder was pressed back into uniform in April 1950 as chairman of the British Joint Services Mission in Washington. He accepted the appointment, stipulating it last for no more than twelve months, because the Americans respected, trusted, and even liked him. His main task was to help translate NATO into a practical military organization. When the Korean War broke out in June 1950, he occupied a key position as a conduit through whom military authorities in Washington and Whitehall could privately explain to each other what they really expected.

To his great pleasure, Tedder learned in November 1950 that he had been elected chancellor of Cambridge University, succeeding Jan Christian Smuts, whom he regarded as the greatest man he ever met. Nothing in Tedder's public life, not even appointment as chief of the air staff, gave him more satisfaction than this elevation, the highest to which a devout Cambridge man can aspire. This news strengthened his determination to resist pressure, American and British, to stay on in Washington. Upon his return to England in May 1951, he gratefully resumed civilian life.

During the last twenty years of his life, Tedder spoke

regularly in debates on defense issues in the House of Lords and vehemently opposed the Anglo-French/Israeli assault on Egypt in October 1956: "A tragic mistake and a folly because it was the wrong action at the wrong time and in the wrong way."

In April 1960 he suffered a stroke in Los Angeles. His recovery was slow, and his ability to write declined. Although he gradually became wheelchair bound, he remained mentally alert and even cheerful.

Under the circumstances, the completion of Tedder's World War memoirs *With Prejudice* (begun in 1962 and published in October 1966) was remarkable. He received essential help from the historian David Dilks, and Zuckerman and other friends offered detailed criticism, but the finished work is Tedder's. He died at home on June 3, 1967. He lived just long enough to know that his book had attracted scholarly as well as popular attention throughout the English-speaking world.

Vincent Orange

Bibliography

Aitken, W. M., ed. *A History of 207 Squadron*, 1984.
S. Cox, S. "An Unwanted Child: the Struggle to Establish a British Bombing Survey," *The Strategic Air War against Germany, 1939–1945: Report of the British Bombing Survey Unit* (1998): xvii–xli.
———, "'The difference between white and black': Churchill, Imperial Politics and Intelligence before the 1941 Crusader Offensive," *Intelligence and National Security* 9 (1994):Davis, R. G. "RAF–AAF Higher Command Structures and Relationships, 1942–45," *Air Power History* 38 (1991): 20–28.
Norris, C. Foxley. "Marshal of the Royal Air Force Lord Tedder," *The War Lords: Military Commanders of the Twentieth Century*, edited by M. Carver (1976): 485–99.

Jackson, W. and Lord Bramall. *The Chiefs: the Story of the United Kingdom Chiefs of Staff.* 1992.

Kent, J. *British Imperial Strategy and the Origins of the Cold War, 1944–49.* 1993.

Kingston-McCloughry, E. J. *The Direction of War: a Critique of the Political Direction and High Command in War.* 1955.

Mierzejewski, A. C. *The Collapse of the German War Economy, 1944–1945: Allied Air Power and the German National Railway.* 1988.

——, "Intelligence and the Strategic Bombing of Germany: the Combined Strategic Targets Committee," *International Journal of Intelligence and Counter–Intelligence* 3 (1989): 83–104.

Orange, V. *Coningham.* 1990.

——, *Tedder: Quietly in Command.* 2003.

Owen, R. *Tedder.* 1952.

Richards, D. *Portal of Hungerford.* 1977.

Ritchie, S. *Industry and Air Power: the Expansion of British Aircraft Production, 1935–1941.* 1997.

Rostow, W. W. *Pre–invasion Bombing Strategy: General Eisenhower's Decision of March 25, 1944.* 1981.

Tedder, Lord [A. W. Tedder]. *With Prejudice: the War Memoirs of Marshal of the Royal Air Force, Lord Tedder.* 1966.

——, *Air Power in War.* 1948.

——, "Air, Land and Sea Warfare," *Journal of the Royal United Service Institution* 91 (1946): 59–68.

——, "The Problem of our Future Security", *RAF Quarterly*, 19 (1948), 8–18.

Terraine, J. *The Right of the Line: the Royal Air Force in the European War, 1939–1945.* 1985.

Zuckerman, Lord. "Marshal of the RAF Lord Tedder (1890–1967): The Politically Sensitive Airman," *Six Men Out of the Ordinary* (1992): 65–98. In *From Apes to Warlords* by S. Zuckerman. 1978. 405–47.

— 1 —

THE UNITIES OF WAR

IT has been well said, " If you wish for peace, understand war."[1] The war of 1939-45 was marked by rapid and immense changes in the technique of warfare, but current developments in science and technology suggest the probability of even more revolutionary changes in the near future. Now more than ever must our understanding of war be sound, up-to-date, and kept up-to-date. War is no longer a series of battles; it is a test of strength, a test not only of the strength of the Armed Forces, but a test of the whole strength of a nation, a test of its moral strength as well as its physical strength, a test of its brains as well as its muscles, a test of its stamina as well as its courage. Step by rapid step science is making that test more severe, more absolute. Our understanding must keep pace with the potentialities of the future, but the essential foundations for that are a proper appreciation of the real nature and scope of modern war and a clear understanding of what happened during the late war.

Expressed in its simplest terms, war is the process by which a nation endeavours to impose its will

[1] *When Britain Goes to War*—by Liddell Hart.

on its opponent. Military operations are merely one of the methods by which a belligerent hopes to achieve his object; they are not an end in themselves. Linked closely with the physical war waged by the armed forces is the political war and the economic war; the political war which aims at weakening morale and authority, the war which the Nazis waged so successfully before the armed conflict broke out; the economic war which aims at starving the enemy war production of its essential materials, the type of war which in the past has been specially appropriate to sea power. Each of these types of warfare has, of course, its reverse aspect; in political warfare, propaganda in many and varied forms is used to raise and maintain the morale of the people; in economic warfare there is the unremitting campaign to improve and increase development and production of all that is essential for the conduct of war, a campaign which is fought in the design shop, in the factories, in the docks, and on the roads and railways. All these varied activities dovetail in with the military operations at sea, in the air, and on land. The better they are balanced and co-ordinated the more economical will be the expenditure of effort, and the greater will be the power generated by the nation at war.

In the late war I think the effectiveness of the machinery for co-ordinating all the national effort was probably one of the main secrets of our ultimate success.

At the outset of a war, time is the supreme

factor. As Mahan puts it : " It behoves countries whose people, like all free peoples, object to paying for large military establishments, to see to it that they are at least strong enough to gain the time to turn the spirit and capacity of their subjects into the new activities which war calls for." A crucial question is : how long will it take a peaceful nation to re-organise and switch over the whole of its national potential to the one supreme task of fighting and winning the war ? In the case of Britain in this last war, although the five years before September, 1939, had seen some useful preparatory work, particularly as regards aircraft development and production and training, I think it is fair to say that it was not until the end of the so-called " phoney war," until we had been shocked out of our apathy by the fall of France and inspired by Mr. Churchill's dynamic leadership, that we really got down to business and to total war. And when we did get down to it we did it properly. Never before in our history have we as a nation been so united both in spirit and in action ; never before have all classes and all ages devoted themselves so utterly to the great national cause : the willing sacrifice of liberties and leisure, of luxuries and of much normally called necessary, the cheerful acceptance of discomforts and danger, the loyal co-operation—all these things build up to an example of national unity rare in history, and also provide proof that a healthy democracy can beat the totalitarian at his own game. By contrast, as I shall discuss later in these lectures, one of the most remarkable facts that has come to light since the end of the war is that, despite all the Nazi talk about total war, it was not until the war had lasted nearly four years that Germany really began to try and utilise her full war potential—and by that time it was too late.

But to return to Mahan : " It behoves countries to see to it that they are at least strong enough to gain the time "—I repeat that—" strong enough to gain the time."

Do not let us forget that the aggressor is also concerned with the time factor ; he is ready, otherwise he would not provoke armed conflict ; he inevitably hopes and plans for a quick decision, since no one would wish for a long war if it could be avoided ; moreover, he wants a decision before his opponent has had time to " turn his capacity into the new activities which war calls for." The peace-loving State, therefore, must not merely have the staying power to hold on until its war potential is fully mobilised ; it must also have the initial strength to withstand the initial shock —intended as that is to be a knock-out in the first round. The initial strength must, moreover be ready at all times. In the late war we fortunately had a fairly protracted period of tension or warning—thanks to the fact that Hitler tried to attain his objective first by means of political warfare—the nerve war in many forms. On the other hand, though some warning period would normally be probable, that warning may be very brief and the initial blow may be a bolt from the blue like the Japanese attack on the U.S. fleet at Pearl Harbour. The United States also were fortunate at the outset of the late war ; they did not have the breathing space afforded to us by the " phoney war " and Munich, but they had the best part of two years' preparation while their war potential was being developed to supply us with materials and munitions. They were also quick to reap the benefits of the technical lessons we learnt in the hard school of war.

One of the features of modern scientific and technical development is that more and more the scales are being weighted in favour of the " Blitzkrieg " : as modern weapons develop, the potentiality of the initial blow tends to grow and grow. More than ever is it necessary to make sure that the lessons of the latest war have been clearly disentangled with judicial objectiveness from the welter of sentimental glamour and blind traditions, professional bias and personal prejudices, and sometimes deliberate misrepresentation, which so often cloak the real truth concerning military operations. We managed to win this latest war —and win it decisively—but it took us nearly half as long again as the previous war, despite our national unity. It is true that the cost of lives to the British Commonwealth and Empire was far lighter in World War II than it was in World War I—just over *one million* casualties compared with over *three millions* ; but the financial cost to the United Kingdom of this last war was

£26,000 millions. There are some awkward questions to be asked to which we must get the sure answers. To what were the astronomical cost and long duration of the war due? How far were they due to the way the political cards were stacked in 1939—due, in other words, to faulty policy in the years between the wars? Was our immense war effort directed into the right channels? Were our forces properly balanced? Did we fight the war in the manner best suited to our special capabilities and limitations? How far were the length and cost of the war due to the general unreadiness at the outset which has so often been typical of " free " people? How far due to military and technical unreadiness for the type of war which actually eventuated?

The technique of warfare is always changing, sometimes drastically; yet I'm afraid one must admit that the military mind is only too often very unreceptive to new ideas and new methods. The chivalrous horror and disgust which the armoured knights of old felt for the vulgar invention of gunpowder was matched not so many years ago by similar righteous disgust at the breach of gentlemanly military etiquette by the introduction of the aeroplane and the bomb. I suspect that even now in some people's minds the bomb is still somewhat disreputable when compared with the bullet and the shell. Now, just when we might reasonably have expected, after some six years of experience of modern war, to be able to sit back and have a quiet stocktaking to see what war nowadays really means and involves, we are faced by the frightening potentialities of the atomic weapon. I say "frightening" deliberately—partly because the potentialities *are* frightening, but also because I am sure it is important for us to be absolutely honest with ourselves about these things. I see that a new phrase has been coined to describe the atomic weapon : it is called a "weapon of mass destruction." I imagine the knights of old had some similar epithets for gunpowder implying that it was an indecent, ungentlemanly, immoral business altogether. I suspect, however, that the true reason for the opposition to the use of gunpowder was fear, fear that it would upset the established order—as in fact it did. I do hope we shall not dress up our attitude towards atomic warfare in any similar camouflage of morality. The history of war affords little hope that nations which are fighting for their lives and beliefs will be restricted in their conduct of the war by moral factors. No. Let us face up frankly to the hard fact that the use of this new weapon is not a question of morality, but is simply and crudely a threat to the very existence of civilisation. It has not been morality but expediency that has governed the use of new weapons, and probably the best safeguard the world can have against the use of the atomic weapon is world-wide knowledge and realisation of its awful potentialities.

We British are often accused of preparing for the last war, or even the last war but one. I think that in some respects and on some occasions there is perhaps a germ of truth in the accusation. Be that as it may, I am quite sure that we cannot afford to do that in these days. The rate of technical development is now so rapid, and the effects of changes in technique so far-reaching, that it may well be fatal to lag behind. For our own security, and for the strength behind U.N.O., we must think in terms of modern war. The last war is not modern, it is out of date.

At the same time there are factors which do not change, or only change very slowly. Geography does not change—though its effect on military operations may be modified by technical changes. Human nature does not change, and national characteristics and temperaments change but slowly. Economic factors, generally speaking, change slowly. These are some of the main factors which determine strategy, and the problem is to arrive at a balanced judgment as to the inter-relationship between the rapidly changing technique and the more constant factors.

Let us go back a stage into the past. Prior to 1914 the solution to the problem of our security was a relatively simple one, readily comprehensible to any thinking man—especially after it had been clearly enunciated by Captain Mahan. For some hundreds of years British trade had spread round the world by sea, new markets had been found, new territories acquired—and with them, new bases established from which British naval craft could protect British trade and, in time of war, deny the sea routes to an enemy. British strength lay in seaborne commerce and British security rested on her naval forces, her world-wide bases and her own insularity. In other words we relied entirely on sea power. In those days Britain could spend as much or as little as she chose on the land campaigns which at frequent intervals have torn Europe asunder. You will remember Bacon's famous dictum : " He that commands the sea is at great liberty and may take as much and as little of the warre as he will, whereas those that be strongest by land, are many times nevertheless at great straits." In 1914 we changed all that, and we entered the lists as a continental power, while at the same time maintaining our position as a maritime power. We soon proved the truth of Bacon's saying and were " at great straits " on two or three occasions. Instead of being able to rely on sea power alone, we were now compelled to raise and maintain a continental army. No longer could we take as little as we liked of the war ; war became a very expensive business in men, money and material.

Then, further to complicate our problems, war spread to the third dimension. The initial rôle of aircraft was merely to be an auxiliary to certain branches of the land and sea forces, but it was not long before thinking men began to see much wider potentialities ahead. The first daylight aeroplane raid on London in 1917 showed the writing on the wall, and a certain wise man called General Smuts reported to the War Cabinet : " The day may not be far off when aerial operations with their devastation of enemy lands and destruction of industrial and populous centres on a vast scale may become the principal operations of war, to which the older forms of military and naval operations may become secondary and subordinate."

General Smuts concluded his report by saying : " It is important that we should not only secure air predominance, but secure it on a very large scale ; and having secured it in this war (1914–18) we should make every effort and sacrifice to maintain it for the future. Air supremacy may in the long run become as important a factor in the defence of the Empire as sea supremacy."

World War I, however, ended before these prophecies could really be put to the test. It was only a handful of far-sighted and determined people who saw what was then the shape of things to come, and it is to them we owe the fact that we could fight and win the Battle of Britain in 1940. Comparatively few, even in the military professions, appreciated what the advent of air power was to mean, not only to the security of this country, but to the conduct of war as a whole. It is true the air was a revolutionary and relatively untried field, but I wonder sometimes how many people understood even the implications of our becoming involved in large-scale land campaigns.

Be that as it may, World War I left us with a number of problems unresolved. By general consent sea power was still our first requirement ; and yet, though our command at sea (in the old sense) had become complete, our battle fleet undefeated, the enemy fleet driven back to harbour ultimately to surrender ignominiously—despite all this, interruption of our sea-borne supplies had brought us nearer a fatal crisis than ever in our previous history : it was obvious that the submarine was a new and major factor, the aeroplane a potential factor, affecting sea power. Clearly some drastic changes were developing in the methods by which command at sea could be secured. Nevertheless, I'm afraid that one must admit that the arrangements for securing command at sea on the outbreak of World War II showed no real change in character from those in force twenty-two years earlier.

On land also there was the unsolved problem of reconciling our peace-time policy of a small professional army for imperial policing with a probable war-time policy of operating a large continental army in Europe. 1939 found us with an army with equipment quite inadequate in quality and quantity and lacking any reserve organisation for expansion to the scale of continental warfare.

In the air, thanks to the far-sighted and determined few, we had the basic organisation which subsequently stood the test of war ; we had, thanks to the breathing space given us, an air defence just adequate to cover the evacuation from Dunkirk and subsequently to win the Battle of Britain. But the other component parts of our air power were at the outset quite inadequate to meet the immediate commitments ; it was practically three years before the principal arm of air power, the Bomber force, became a power in the world ; the air forces for the defence of our overseas bases, for tactical support of land operations, for taking part in the fight for command at sea— all these were totally inadequate at the outset. Moreover, inadequate as were the air forces for support of the army, the army provision for support of the air—A.A. and ground defence of air bases, provision of engineers for airfields, etc.—was even more inadequate.

I feel we must frankly admit that after World War I we as a nation completely failed to see war as a single problem in which the strategy, the tactics, and the technique of sea, land and air warfare respectively are inevitably and closely interlocked. There were a few voices crying in the wilderness, but generally speaking the unities of land, sea, and air of which I have spoken were maintained in the narrowest and most exclusive sense and not—as I feel they should—as parts of a greater and comprehensive unified national defence. It was argued that the war at sea was the exclusive preserve of the Royal Navy, and that land operations were the preserve of the army ; by many the very existence of air power was denied ; combined operations were literally a no-man's-land. Easy criticism perhaps. But criticism is needed. We cannot afford to make mistakes. We must subject the events of the late war to a searching objective analysis ; we must look behind the battles and the headlines ; we must search out to see what really happened behind the things that made news ; we must analyse the mistakes and the successes on both sides ; see where we went wrong and why ; where we went right and how. And then, for our future security, we must look *forward from* the past and its lessons, not *back to* the past.

Sometimes I feel we have a tendency to concentrate too much on our successes and our enemies' failures and consequently to draw our lessons too much from the final stages of war. I suggest there is danger in this. In the latter stages of a war, after some years of lavish expenditure of money, material, and man-power in the equipment and manning of all arms of the fighting services, military problems have a way of becoming relatively easy of solution. Awkward questions of relative priority will always arise, but in the final stages of a war they rarely have the critical urgency they have at the outset. The campaign is immensely simplified for the Commander if he knows he can count on a blank cheque. Surely it is the problems of the early stages of the war which we should study. Those are the difficult problems ; those are the practical problems which we and every democratic nation have to solve. There were no big battalions or blank cheques then. Here is the real and vital test of our defence policies. It is at the outset of war that time is the supreme factor. Were we, in September, 1939, " at least strong enough to gain the time " ? Is there not some justification in the accusation that Abyssinia, Austria, and finally Czechoslovakia were succes-

sively sacrificed because we were not strong enough?
I suspect that most thinking people in this country
felt deep shame about Munich ; I know I did ;
but I well remember the overwhelming relief
which, from the military point of view, one felt :
Munich gave us that most precious thing—time—
but some people would say we bought it at the
cost of our honour. Munich gave us a year, and
then the " phoney war " gave us another eight
months. Despite all this, the Battle of Britain
in 1940 was a very close call. Could we have won
it in 1939 ? I think not. That providential eight
months made the Battle of Britain possible and
saved Britain and much else besides. In April,
1938, the estimates of the three Defence Departments for the ensuing year totalled £343¼ millions,
with an additional £8½ millions for A.R.P. services ;
yet at the time of Munich this country was virtually
defenceless. It was three years before the tide even
began to turn ; three years during which we were
fighting rearguard actions to protect our interests
throughout the world ; three years of military
operations undertaken with forces which were un-
balanced and inadequate. Only in the air were
we beginning to recover the initiative. It is under
these conditions that the mistakes, whether of
policy or of technique, stand out most clearly.
In the subsequent years of military plenty, successes due in no small measure to overwhelming
material superiority, inevitably dazzle the eye so
that the mistakes cannot easily be seen. Indeed,
the availability of almost unlimited resources has

in itself an element of danger in more than one
direction. When the purse strings are loose the
thinking is apt to be loose. Financial stringency
leads to careful budgeting, and, conversely, if our
military thought draws its conclusions solely from
the lush days of the last phase of the war and
directs its policy for the future on that basis, then
we certainly shall not be prepared for the lean
days which we should undoubtedly have to face
at the outset were another war to eventuate. This
is true not only of tactics, but also of overall defence
policy. It would be a singularly futile business for
us, having been brought uncomfortably near bankruptcy by two wars on the blank cheque basis,
to complete the journey to the bankruptcy court
by uncritical defence expenditure in peace.

We simply must get the whole business of warfare and national defence back on to a sound
economical basis, and we must clear our minds
as to what would be our aim in any future war.
I believe that, in future, war will inevitably be
total war and world-wide ; but that does not
necessarily imply that we should conduct our share
of such a war on similar lines to those we followed
in World Wars I and II. Personally, I do not
see how we could survive winning a third victory
like the two previous ones. What shall it profit
us if we win the victory and lose our civilisation ?
I am sure we must be far more selective in the
allocation of our national effort to military defence.
We must pay far more attention to the principle
of economy of force—and when I say " economy "

I do not mean the false economy got by doing things on the cheap, but the economy which comes from efficiency, the economy which results from keeping every component part of the national war machine properly balanced in relation to the rest of the machine—the economy, moreover, which organises the armed forces for speed and quick decision. Nearly 500 years B.C. Sun Tzu wrote : " There is no instance of a country having been benefited from prolonged warfare." The wholesale destruction resulting from the slogging matches of the twentieth century have brought modern civilisation perilously near disintegration.

The attainment of true economy will not be easy. We are shackled by the past, and never has the future been more difficult to divine. What we must do is to discard quite ruthlessly ideas, traditions, and methods which have not stood the test of economy. Each of the fighting services must discard old shibboleths and outworn traditions, go to the scientists and technicians for all they can possibly give in the way of speed, mobility, and economy, and then develop the whole time with an eye on the other two members of the team in co-operation, *not* in competition. Couple this with the mutual frankness and mutual faith which brought success in the war and we shall get what we need—a united, efficient, and economical armed force : not an embryo Goliath which would take years to come to maturity after the outbreak of war, but a fully-grown David, ready to act swiftly and decisively as one of the world's policemen.

— 2 —

AIR SUPERIORITY

I HAVE spoken of land, sea, and air warfare as separate, yet closely inter-related. Everyone recognises the separate unity of sea and land warfare respectively—in the past very often an exclusive and separatist unity. It took men like Pitt to see and utilise the relationship between the two. Even in this war I have occasionally met soldiers and sailors, and even some airmen, who completely failed to appreciate the close relationship between their respective operations. In the early days I met many more (but naturally not airmen) who denied the very existence of such a thing as air warfare, and I'm afraid that, to this day, there are not a few people who not only are ignorant of the vital dependence of all surface operations on the progress of the war in the air, but also deny the separate unity of air warfare.

One of my objections to the title of these lectures was that it might give the impression that I regarded air power as something quite apart from sea power and land power. I do not. In my view, air power is an immense entity in itself, but it is interlocked with sea and land power, and all three are interdependent. Another objection I had was that " air power " may have different meanings for different people : that is certainly the case as regards the corresponding phrase " sea power." To some people sea power means merely naval forces, whereas to others—the majority—it has always meant the ability to use and keep in use the sea communications, coupled with the ability to deny them to the enemy. While this is traditionally correct, it is not wholly complete as a definition to-day. As you will note, there are two thoughts in the term " sea power " : one is that of command at sea, and the other the exercise of sea power, or rather the use of sea communications. In the fight for command at sea, and denying its use to the enemy, air forces now join as partners with naval forces, and, as Mr. Bryant recently pointed out, it is conceivable that this command in the future may be secured mainly by air forces in some form or another. On the other hand, so far as we can judge at present, it does not seem likely that the air will play the primary part in controlling the actual use we make of sea communications. This will perhaps indicate some of the termino-logical difficulties in selecting titles for lectures. My use of the phrase " air power " is in a similar sense to the traditional definition of " sea power " ; that is to say, air power is the ability to use the air spaces for offensive, defensive, and supply services, and to deny their use to an enemy. Air forces, civil transport, air bases, communications for control and direction, radar and radio facilities, aircraft and engine industries—all these are components of air power. It is the exercise of air power that I want to examine. I want, briefly, in the light of the experience we have gained during the last war, to try and clear our minds as to the influence of air power on modern warfare.

British sea power has been based on two factors —geography and national temperament. Great Britain is an island, and the British are a race of shopkeepers, tradesmen and travellers. Trade and commerce have been in our blood ; our commerce has had to go by sea and its security has been— and is—vital to our very existence, and consequently command at sea has been a pre-requisite of our national defence. In war, so long as we maintained command at sea, we were covered not only against the major threat of the severing of our supply lines, but also against the other threat of invasion. So long as sea warfare was only carried on by surface ships, the problem of exercising and maintaining command at sea was solved on the simple formula of frigates and ships of the line, or, in modern phraseology, cruisers backed by the main fleet. It is true that the French *guerre de course* was at times a considerable nuisance, but never more than that. Traditional methods were, however, no solution to the problem that faced us when the Germans developed the *guerre de course* into the submarine campaign in 1917. Still less were they a solution for the even more dangerous problems of this late war.

Impinging upon and gradually percolating throughout sea power there was now the new factor—air power. You will remember how in 1917 General Smuts, in one of those flashes of far-seeing wisdom so typical of that great man, said : " Air supremacy may in the long run become as important a factor in the defence of the Empire as sea supremacy." It was remarkable how few people in the early stages of this last war, even those in positions of authority, realised what the introduction and development of this new three-dimensional warfare was to mean to war as a whole. The lesson as to what it meant was only driven home in those early days at the cost of much blood and bitterness. Command at sea remained, as it still remains, vital to our very existence, but the forces required to exercise that command had changed in character. We were to find out in the hard school of war that without air supremacy, or, as we now say, " air superiority," sea power could no longer be exercised ; and, without air superiority, air power itself could not be exercised. We were also to find that, given air superiority, air forces themselves could be the decisive factor in securing and maintaining command at sea. But the outstanding lesson of the late war was that air superiority is the pre-requisite to all war-winning operations, whether at sea, on land, or in the air. In other words, in order even to begin to wage war successfully, it is necessary to arrive at the situation in which the enemy air opposition is unable to interfere effectively with our own operations—that is what we mean by air superiority.

The opening moves of the air-sea war in 1939 were in accordance with the best naval tradition. On the first day of the war photographic reconnaissance of the German Fleet was carried out by one R.A.F. Blenheim, and the following day, in bad weather, a force of twenty-nine R.A.F. bombers attacked enemy warships lying off the entrance to the Kiel Canal. Between then and the end of the year four more daylight bombing attacks were carried out against the German Fleet. The numbers of aircraft available were small (the largest raid was 18—the first) and the losses, mostly at the hands of enemy fighters, were heavy— between 25 per cent. and 50 per cent. It is interesting to note that the orders were that the ships were not to be attacked if they were tied up alongside, lest German soil should be hit. On the last daylight raid the ships were tied up alongside, so the whole operation was abortive, though expensive. In the meantime the enemy had carried out similar operations against our naval vessels at Rosyth and Scapa. These attacks were also on a similar scale, ineffective and expensive. These operations against the opposing fleets, ineffective though they were, were the first clear warnings of what General Smuts called " air supremacy " was going to mean to sea power.

They had, however, confirmed the soundness of the basic doctrine which had been evolved at the end of World War I. Air superiority was the pre-requisite to any successful air operation—and now here was the warning that perhaps General Smuts was right.

Our operations against the German Fleet showed up one respect in which we had been wrong. It had been thought that, though the bomber could not, by its very nature, be as fast as the fighter, yet it could cope with the fighter provided it had sufficient speed and effective defensive armament. The heavy casualties suffered by the raids off Kiel and Wilhelmshaven showed that this was not the case, and from that time on till late in the war the great bulk of our bomber operations over Germany were at night. The fact was that we could not operate bombers by day unescorted over the German coast in any conditions of light and weather which would allow of accurate bombing. The whole of our available fighter strength was taken up in interceptor fighters for home defence, and we had, and at that time could have, no fighters fit for long-range escort to the bombers. We had no means of securing even the temporary and local air superiority without which the bombers could not effectively operate.

The fight for air superiority is not a straightforward issue like a naval battle or a land battle ; it is not even a series of combats between fighters ; it is frequently a highly complex operation which may involve any or all types of aircraft. It is a campaign rather than a battle, and there is no absolute finality to it so long as any enemy aircraft are operating. It may be very local and temporary,

34

i.e. covering a specific operation, or it may be widespread and sustained as it was in the final phase of the war in Europe.

I think that one reason why people have found it difficult to understand is that it is most effective when the operations to secure and maintain superiority are not visible to those who are benefiting from it. In the early days of inexperience and misunderstanding many of our soldiers thought that if there were no British fighters over their heads the Air Force was letting them down. The normal request was for an " air umbrella "—a method of employing fighters which is both the most extravagant and normally the least effective ; a method, moreover, which, if persisted in, is a sure way of losing any degree of air superiority you may have. The speed and flexibility of air operations puts a premium on gaining and keeping the initiative. Of air warfare, if anything, is the old adage true—that offence is the best defence.

The Germans had, at the beginning of the war, a simple formula for getting air superiority at the very outset. The initial blow in a campaign was an all-out surprise attack by bombers, dive-bombers, and fighters on the opponents' air bases, sometimes accompanied by parachute and airborne landings ; the second stage was destruction of the aircraft factories. This formula worked to perfection in Poland, where the Polish Air Force was virtually destroyed on the first day, and again both in Norway and in Holland. When they followed the same formula against us in

Northern France surprise was lacking, but they inflicted considerable losses in one or two instances, since our airfields had only light defences and the warning organisation was inadequate. The real test came, however, with the opening of the Battle of Britain. After preliminary feelers on coastal shipping, airfields and radar stations were their targets in the first round. At three or four airfields more or less serious damage was done though few aircraft were destroyed. There were, however, ample alternative airfields from which our fighters could continue to operate and they were little affected. At the same time the organisation for warning and control of the defence was efficient and the proportion of successful interceptions was high. Moreover, the British fighters were far superior in fire power and had the advantage in speed. Enemy losses were high. Then, though it must have been clear that our fighter defence was still fully effective, the Germans proceeded to the next step in their plan, the docks and ports. Then some spasmodic and ineffective attacks on airfields further inland, and a few attacks on aircraft factories. These stages in the German campaign were not really in accord with the formula for air superiority which had been so successful before. Still less was the final one of wholesale attacks on London. The original formula provided for the gaining of absolute air superiority as the essential first step, by knocking out the opposing air force first on its airfields and then in its factories. But against Britain the

Germans failed to persist in these first-phase operations. As a result, the fight for air superiority was fought in the air. The battle focused on and round the German bomber formations, and in this contest the Germans were beaten. I have already referred to the superior fire power of the eight-gun British fighters. The enemy also suffered from the lack of any real effective defensive armament in their bombers. They were in fact not equipped or trained so as to be ready to fight for air superiority. The Battle of Britain was lost and won before they could rectify their mistake.

The campaign in Greece and Crete is a vivid contrast. Our Air Force, after its successful winter campaign in Greece against the Italians, had moved up to the east and north with the army advance. The airfields they had to occupy were small, and there were no engineers to enlarge them or to provide dispersal or protection ; there was no effective warning organisation and virtually no A.A. defence. Skill and gallantry could inflict heavy casualties on superior numbers in the air, but were of little avail when the bases were defenceless. The normal German formula worked like a charm, and soon only a handful of the aircraft of R.A.F. Greece were left to retire to Crete. On Crete there were three airfields and two more in the making. For four months defensive preparations had been in hand, but little effective had been done. Arms and equipment were short in those days, and even picks and shovels were lacking. Some defences were improvised during

the short breathing space between the evacuation
of Greece and the German assault, but it was
too late for them to be effective. Meantime the
German aircraft—fighters, bombers, and transports—assembled on fields in Southern Greece
and on the islands in a half-moon facing Crete,
and little could be done about them. A Beau-
fighter squadron, just arrived at Malta, did a round
trip, staging at Crete, and destroyed a dozen or
more Ju. 52's lined up on one of the Athens airfields;
Wellingtons from Egypt attacked some of the airfields in the Dodecanese ; but these were mere
pinpricks. Nothing more was possible. When
the German assault on Crete began—true to
formula by attacks on the three occupied airfields
—the air defence of the island consisted of Hurricanes and Swordfish. Six days of such attacks
and it was clearly futile to try and maintain any
aircraft on the island. A few gallant and desperate
attempts made from the Western Desert 300 miles
away by Hurricanes carrying fixed external tanks
could not really affect the issue, and the enemy,
operating in large numbers at short range from
secure bases, had complete air superiority in his
hands, virtually without having to fight for it.
Crete fell in twelve days.

In the Western Desert, where the numerical
strengths of the opposing air forces were approximately the same, air superiority over the enemy
was secured and maintained by a wide and constantly changing variety of operations. These
operations, which included various forms of attack

on airfields, fighter sweeps, attacks on supplies (especially fuel), and attacks on repair bases, were intensified periodically to coincide with particular land operations or movements of convoys ; but they were with one exception always offensive and never entirely relaxed. The exception was a standing patrol over the Coastal convoys which supplied Tobruk when it was invested. Small though these patrols were, they were relatively expensive in effort, and they were thoroughly bad for the morale and efficiency of the pilots. They were, however, essential, if only as a deterrent.

There is in fact no rule-of-thumb solution to the problem of securing air superiority, no simple formula. The " fight for air superiority " is in fact " air warfare " expressed in other words and, even more than sea warfare and land warfare, it has an almost infinite variety. There is nothing absolute about air superiority—so long as the enemy can operate any aircraft. It is a situation which, except in such exceptional cases as the Blitz on Poland, develops gradually and can only be judged by the results which flow from it. Since it is a compound of so many factors—command, morale, training, numbers, technical performance, reserves and supplies, to mention a few of the main factors—it is not capable of any precise or mathematical assessment. Orders of battle may be a very misleading criterion. I remember coming up against this myself in 1941 just before the opening of one of the earlier Desert offensives. The authorities at home were anxious, for certain

reasons of which I was not aware, to be able to
assure the world that the army would have ample
" air support," and quoted figures of comparative
aircraft strengths to show that we had numerical
superiority over the Germans. The figures quoted
were a convenient selection and did not in my opinion
give an accurate state of the aircraft I would be
able to employ in the Desert campaign, or of the
enemy aircraft based in various parts of the Eastern
Mediterranean with which I would have to cope.
I had some difficulty in getting across with my
firmly-held opinion that we could and would deal
quite satisfactorily with the enemy air forces
whatever the figures of strength were supposed
to be. Since I did feel that the figures were not
what mattered, we were able to come to a com-
promise which satisfied all parties. Air superiority
is a subtle question; before one has seen the
results which flow from it I think one can only
sense it. You may say this is nebulous basis on
which to launch major combined operations such
as the Sicily and Normandy landings—for which
air superiority was an essential pre-requisite—
certainly nothing like as satisfactory as an enemy
order of battle ! I could not help feeling a certain
sympathy for my soldier and sailor colleagues in
the earlier days who could not understand why,
before their operations began, I could only say
I " thought " and " felt " the air situation would
be all right, and would give no precise guarantees.

Yet even though one " felt " the air situation
was satisfactory one must admit to a certain

degree of anxiety until the proof of the pudding was manifest. The invasion of Sicily was a typical case in point, even though this was the beginning of the days of plenty. The intensive operations to clear the air for the invasion went on for some six weeks before D Day. Ports, rail centres in Sicily and South Italy, and airfields, especially in Sicily, had been the main target. Originally there had been only some nineteen airfields on the island, but as the threat of invasion loomed nearer and nearer satellite airstrips began to spread across the country in a most disturbing manner—I remember one airfield which by D Day had no less than eleven satellites—and despite the thorough way in which our attacks (especially those of the American bombers) had covered the strips and dispersal areas one could not help wondering if, when the show-down came on D Day, we should find that we really had done the job. It would have needed only a small surviving enemy force to do immense damage during the initial landings. The fact that when D Day came we found the enemy air forces had been paralysed is a matter of history. Their order of battle had given an entirely false impression of their true state.

There was a similar element of the unknown prior to the landings in Normandy, in spite of the fact that since 1940 allied superiority had gradually extended from the British coast, over the coastal sea routes, across to the shores of Europe and finally to some extent over parts of Europe itself.

How unknown was the degree of air superiority we had attained is shown by the fact that prior to D Day it was estimated that the Luftwaffe would carry out between 600 and 700 sorties per day over the area of the landings ; whereas in fact (except for sudden bursts of activity when up to 350 sorties were flown in a day) they were unable to maintain a daily average of more than 200.

The other difficulty which frequently arises about air superiority is that of identifying, even in retrospect, exactly which factors contributed towards success. This is particularly true of the operations over Europe. In September, 1940, Germany had 1,162 fighters, and 1,871 bombers compared with Britain's 888 fighters and 576 bombers. In September, 1944, German strength in Western Europe was 2,473 fighters and 209 bombers compared with Allied strength of 4,523 fighters (of which the majority were employed as fighter-bombers) and 2,682 bombers (of which the majority were four-engined bombers) (*see Diagram No.* 1). During that quarter of 1944 German monthly fighter production was very considerably higher than the combined British and American fighter production (of which only a proportion was in fact allocated to the European theatre). Yet by this time the Western Allies had almost absolute air superiority over the Reich. These figures provide, I am sure, one of the key answers to the question : " Why did the Luftwaffe fail ? " Step by step, after losing the Battle of

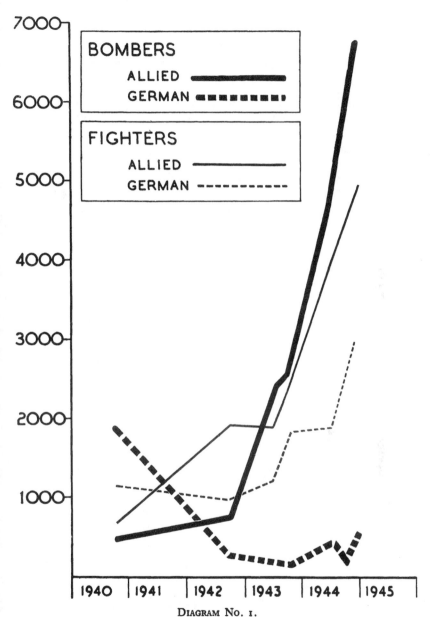

DIAGRAM No. 1.
COMPARATIVE STRENGTHS OF OPERATIONAL AIRCRAFT
DURING BATTLE OF BRITAIN AND ON WESTERN FRONT.

Britain, the Germans had been forced back more and more on the defensive, and they never regained the initiative. More and more was their effort diverted to passive defence—fighters, A.A. and radar defences, A.R.P. measures, etc. More and more did their striking force, the bombers—the dynamic element in their Air Force—fade away. How completely it had atrophied was shown by the futility of their short-lived attempt to stage a come-back at London early in 1944. As a German staff officer expressed it in a lecture in Berlin at the beginning of 1944 : " The decisive battle with the Anglo-American air forces is being fought out over our vital living space."

I emphasise this point because it is a principle fundamental to any understanding of air power. An air force composed of fighters alone is not an air force and is not a defence ; as well have naval ships without guns, or armies without artillery. The fighter and the bomber, the guard and the punch, are complementary. The bomber operations, though unseen, are as vital to the defence of the country as the visible operations of the fighters. This was proved true in the late war. Are future developments likely to affect the principle ? In my view all the possible developments we can now see only serve to reinforce the principle. Very greatly increased bomber speeds will immensely increase the difficulties of providing adequate warning and effective interception, and indeed the fighter's superiority of speed over the bomber (upon which its effectiveness in defence primarily depends) may well dwindle to almost nothing. The most effective defence against air attack is to stop it at its source, and in future it may become the only way ; it is certainly the only method of dealing with the rocket. The only decisive air superiority is that established over the enemy country.

I believe this unbalance of the Luftwaffe to have been, in the end, one of the main causes of their loss of air superiority and of Germany losing the war. It was, I believe, a symptom of deep-seated misconceptions. I have already said the Germans were not equipped or trained to fight for air superiority. Nor were they equipped or trained to exercise air power in a strategic sense, and as an incidental result they were unable to force the fight for air superiority back from their own skies. It is quite clear from all the evidence that Hitler and the German General Staff thought essentially in terms of land warfare. They failed to understand air power even more completely than they failed as regards sea power. The Luftwaffe was in their eyes merely an auxiliary to the ground forces. Admittedly the enemy air force had to be knocked out first, but that was only a brief introductory affair—for the invasion, the R.A.F. was to be knocked out of Southern England in four days !

It is remarkable that, despite the clear lessons of the Battle of Britain, Germany embarked on the Russian war with her air policy unchanged. No serious attempt was made to increase aircraft production or press on the development of new types. It is true that in a directive of July, 1941, Hitler laid down his policy as follows : " The military domination of Europe after the defeat of Russia will enable the strength of the army to be considerably reduced in the near future. Naval armament must be restricted to those measures which have a direct connection with the war against England. The main effort will be shifted to the air force, which must be greatly increased in strength." The " defeat of Russia " did not materialise, and by the end of 1942, at Stalingrad and in the Mediterranean theatre, the Luftwaffe had suffered blows from which they never recovered. In a desperate and futile attempt to relieve von Paulus's army at Stalingrad the Luftwaffe were recklessly, and I feel ignorantly, flung into an operation for which they were quite unsuited, and suffered losses from which their bomber and transport forces never recovered. Even training aircraft were, on Hitler's orders, thrown into the land battle. In the Mediterranean theatre I watched, not without satisfaction, Kesselring fritter away the Luftwaffe's dwindling stock of trained and experienced aircrews in a series of ineffective and dispersed operations. It is true he gave us a headache at Malta, but it cost him dearly, and he got no long-term dividends. What with lack of understanding and direction in Berlin, and misuse and waste at the battle fronts, it is not surprising that not only did the technical efficiency of the Luftwaffe deteriorate, but also morale began to fail. The transfer in the winter of 1942-43 of 200,000 trained men from the Luftwaffe to the Army can scarcely have improved morale in the Luftwaffe. Suicide was apparently a popular item in the Nazi code, but when one finds the suicide rate in the Luftwaffe rising from a modest forty-five a month in 1941 to seventy a month in 1943, and seventy-five a month in 1944, it becomes evident that something had gone wrong—a conclusion which is confirmed by the suicides of the Chief of Air Staff (Jeschonnek) and of Udet, the Head of Development.

An air force is, I suppose, by reason of the nature of its work, a highly-strung and temperamental body. Any fluctuations in its morale have immediate effect on the efficiency of its operations. It is extremely sensitive to any misdirection. If I had been in Jeschonnek's shoes I think my reaction would have been murderous rather than suicidal. When it is facing heavy wastage in war, it depends for its continued health and morale on a high standard of training by first-class experienced instructors. The Luftwaffe suffered in both quality and quantity. The experienced aircrew, who should have been used as instructors, were thrown away in profitless operations, and shortage of oil curtailed training more and more until, in 1944, even operations in the field were being limited by oil shortages. To quote one example, the hours of training given to fighter pilots, which had been slightly higher than that given to R.A.F pilots in 1939-40, gradually dwindled by mid-

1944 to less than a half of what they had been, and a third of ours. Ours had increased in 1942 and then remained steady. The Allied offensive against the German synthetic oil plants in the spring of 1944 had catastrophic results (*see Diagram No. 2*) : in August, 1944, when the invasion of Europe was in full tide, only day fighters actually operating against Allied raids were allowed unrestricted flying. In November many Luftwaffe units were grounded for lack of fuel, and in the spring of 1945 all remaining fuel stocks were exhausted, distribution had stopped owing to the paralysis of transportation, and the Luftwaffe was grounded.

It may appear from what I have said that I am giving most of the credit for the defeat of the Luftwaffe to the German High Command. There is no doubt that Hitler and his gang did, by their mishandling of their air force, contribute most usefully to the Allied cause. But, in any fight, one contestant is as good as his opponent allows him to be, and in this particular case, once the Blitzkrieg had been frustrated, the enemy were pushed back and kept back on the defensive. As a German staff report expressed it in 1944 : " At the beginning of the war the operations of the G.A.F. determined the character of events ; the initiative has now, however, since 1941, been in the hands of the enemy." I shall be discussing the strategic air offensive and its effect on the war as a whole in a later lecture, but in general, of course, the victory in the air was one of its

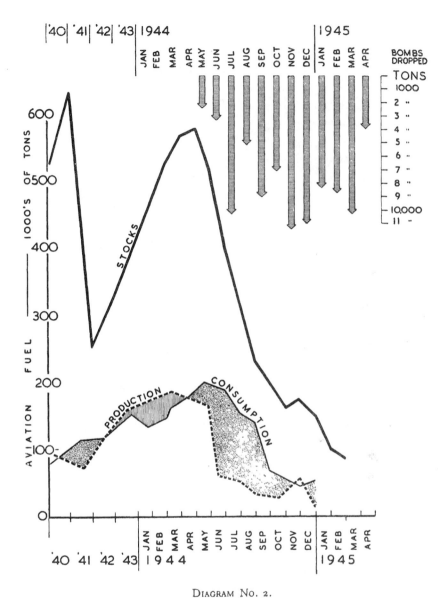

DIAGRAM No. 2.

AVIATION GASOLINE

STOCKS: CONSUMPTION: PRODUCTION AND BOMBS ON
OIL PLANTS.

most important by-products. It *compelled* the Luftwaffe to fight over Germany's "vital living space" by night and by day. Any attempt to differentiate between the various phases of the strategic operations in their effect on the Luftwaffe would be misleading. For example : despite the operations against the German fighter production (operation "Point Blank") which caused concentrated destruction at the bulk of the key fighter factories early in 1944, the fighter production went up far higher than ever before—yet the Luftwaffe grew steadily weaker. When asked to explain this apparent anomaly, Speer, who was Minister of Production and quite the ablest man in authority, remarked : "The answer to that was simple—the Allies destroyed the aircraft as soon as they were made." I have already referred to the catastrophic effect of the offensive against oil production—but that took place in May and June, 1944, and the Luftwaffe had been going down hill long before.

In the final phase of the war, during and after the invasion, they were harried from pillar to post, on the ground, when taking off and landing, and when trying to assemble. In the words of the Commander of the German Fighter Force, the fighting degenerated into a Wild West show put on by the Allies. When the debacle came it was complete, but it was only the climax to a long and bitter struggle, a long-drawn-out battle of wits by day and by night, in fair weather and foul, in tactics and technique : each aspect of it, whether military or technical, is worth a detailed study. The

German Air Force was beaten on all counts : in command and direction, in strategy and tactics, in technique and morale, in quality and quantity ; but it was not a quickly won or easy victory. One sometimes hears it said that the air battle must be won first, before land or sea operations can take place ; that can be misleading : air superiority must be established, and the greater the degree of that superiority the better, but the air battle is continuous, and when it is won the war is all but won.

I think I can best conclude this lecture by quoting again General Smuts's conclusions, arrived at almost thirty years ago when aircraft were still bird-cages of wood and wire : " It is important for the winning of the war that we should not only secure air predominance, but secure it on a very large scale." In World War II we followed his advice, but it took us over three years to do it effectively.

In my two remaining lectures I propose to examine the exercise of air power which air superiority made possible, but before leaving to-day's subject it is perhaps of interest to note that out of the battle of wits humanity will get some real benefits. The struggle to defeat and utilise the weather; the incessant contest between the scientific and technical staffs of both sides to provide measure and counter-measure to improve or confuse navigation by radio and radar; the intense pressure on the design and development of aircraft and engines to improve performance in speed, range, load-carrying and safety—all these war-time activities will pay a handsome dividend for civil aviation. This is not to say that war is worth while, but merely that there is some very valuable salvage to be recovered from it.

— 3 —

AIR POWER IN RELATION TO
SEA POWER

EVEN though there are many who still do not appreciate the full implications of air power, I think everyone will go along with me so far as to agree on the need for air superiority. Air superiority is, however, merely a means towards the end ; it is the state in which the exercise of air power becomes possible. It is when one comes to the use of air power that one begins to meet the misconceptions and consequent disagreements which still linger. It is the old question of the seen and unseen wars. Enemy air interference with our own surface operations is seen and is very real ; consequently superiority in the air over our land and sea forces, so as to prevent that interference, is obviously a very desirable thing. But when it comes to operations which are literally right off the map the outlook tends to be different. The old saying " out of sight out of mind " is apt to apply. I propose, therefore, to examine briefly some examples of the effect of air power on the exercise of land and, especially, sea power.

I have already referred to the initial air exchanges

at Scapa and Kiel in 1939 ; ineffective though they were, they were the writing on the wall which was underlined when the German air attacks on our coastal shipping began to inflict quite trouble-some bother and interference. Air power was clearly going to have a real influence on the exercise of sea power. Despite our great superiority over the Germans in surface ships, even our coastal traffic was no longer secure, and our fleet no longer secure in its own bases.

The German occupation of Denmark and Norway provided some bitter lessons for us, but it also gave some warnings to the enemy had he been able to see them. On the old pattern of amphibious war, the German attack on Norway would appear to have offered us a priceless oppor-tunity of exercising sea power : a coast-line vulner-able at many points to sea-borne attack, a country with limited land communications dependent very largely on sea communications, our own main advanced naval base placed right athwart the enemy's sea-route to all but the southern tip of Norway. We seized the opportunity. Six days after the launching of the German attack we landed somewhat improvised expeditions at two places in Central and at one place in Northern Norway with a view to securing Trondheim and Narvik, which had already been occupied by the enemy by sea and air. But from there on little went right—something was fundamentally out of gear in our operations ; something in the conduct of war had changed. The German occupation had been carried out by relatively small bodies of men conveyed by sea under disguise, supported and reinforced by airborne forces and supplied by air ; airfields had been neutralised and occupied by air, and air forces had been established in Denmark and Norway. The enemy columns, in addition to being reinforced and supplied by air, were given active direct support, and our disembarkation ports and supply shipping were subjected to repeated attack which caused grave losses and severe disorganisation. The Luftwaffe had complete air superiority in Central Norway. The attempt to operate some Gladiators lacking essential ground crews and equipment, with no A.A. defence, lacking even an airfield, and forced to try and operate from a frozen lake, which, within a few hours, was hopelessly pitted with bomb holes—this was the occasion for a wonderful display of gallantry by the handful of pilots concerned ; but, like the cavalry feat at Balaclava, this was the sort of thing which Bosquet would have termed 'magnificent—but not war.' Nor could our carriers or our shore-based aircraft in Great Britain redress the balance ; the vulnerability of the former, and the limited range of the latter, ruled them out as an effective counter.

Further north, round Narvik, affairs were somewhat better, since we had time to make one usable air-strip and operate two fighter squadrons, which were able, during their brief stay, to establish local air superiority over Narvik, though they were not able entirely to stop the air supply on which the

German forces at Narvik depended. Whether or not it would have been possible, at any reasonable price, to maintain forces in Northern Norway must remain a matter of conjecture, for our continental campaign had, to use Bacon's phrase, " brought us to great straits " in France and Belgium, and the evacuation of the Narvik area began while the evacuation of Dunkirk was at its height. A tragic footnote to Norway was added when the two fighter squadrons, having flown off successfully on to the carrier, were lost when the *Glorious* was sunk, with practically all hands, by German surface forces. Apart from our actual losses during the Norwegian campaign, we were to pay a heavy price throughout the war for our failure. Germany now had an open door to the Atlantic, her vital supplies through Northern Norway were secure, her air bases now half encircled Britain, and we were to find to our cost that even the sea route to Russia was precarious. Despite her inferior naval strength, Germany was now able to contest seriously our exercise of sea power ; given air superiority, air forces were now clearly able to take an effective hand in securing command at sea.

The lessons were there, as clearly to be seen by the enemy as they were by us, and indeed Jodl, then Chief of Operations, reported, two days after our evacuation, " The Luftwaffe proved to be the decisive factor in the success of the operation." But I suspect that at that time the enemy only appreciated the defensive value of the air in relation to the sea, and failed to see its potentialities as an active force. There was, in the British air operations, in addition a warning, perhaps only a hint for the future, which I think also went unnoticed by the enemy. Before the German attack was launched a number of large movements of shipping were observed by our air reconnaissance. The main movement up the Kattegat was unseen—we could not penetrate so far. But four nights after the German initial assault, Bomber Command laid mines in the Great Belt ; a small operation which so far as we know paid no direct dividends, small as the cloud the size of a man's hand—but, fortunately, Britain learnt the lesson.

Four and a half years later, when the enemy urgently needed to withdraw divisions from Norway in order to bolster up the crumbling Western Front, special shipping was allocated for troop transport across the short sea passage from Oslo to northern Denmark ; enough ships were allocated to move between two and three divisions a month—in December, 1944, fourteen ships had been detailed for the job. By March, the actual rate of movement, thanks to the losses imposed by air attack and air mining, had dwindled to barely a division in six weeks, and by April the movement was negligible. At one stage only one ship was operating on the route.

This was air power over-riding sea power with a vengeance. It was, however, only a climax to a gradual process, in which our air forces had more and more been bringing economic pressure on the enemy by attacking his coastal trade—in other words, sea blockade exercised by air. Germany's coastal trade, though important, was not vital to her war effort ; consequently the effort directed against it was not given a high priority, either for air or naval forces. Nevertheless, the scale of attack gradually increased, as British air superiority (helped by improving aircraft performance and growing strength) stretched further and further across the seas. It is not possible here to describe in detail the development of the campaign which, by the end of 1944, virtually brought German trade with Scandinavia to a standstill. It was a campaign in which tactics and technique were continually developing ; it involved all R.A.F. Commands—Fighter Command, Coastal Command, Bomber Command—and, in the extreme Northern waters, carrier-borne aircraft ; it involved the bomb, the rocket, the torpedo, and the mine, each and all employed in the conditions appropriate to each weapon. In their consideration of enemy shipping losses over the area of the Baltic and the North-West European seaboard north of the Straits of Dover, the interdepartmental Enemy Shipping Losses Assessment Committee, which functioned throughout the war, reached the conclusion that of a total of 2,471 enemy ships sunk and damaged, 289 fell to surface and under-water vessels ; and the remainder— over 88 per cent.—to aircraft (either by direct attack or by air-sea mining). Relating as they do to *numbers* of ships rather than tonnages, these figures are, of course, inclined to over-rate the value of small-ship casualties, though it must be remembered that many of these small ships were Flak ships and escort vessels. I cannot vouch for the absolute accuracy of the figures themselves, as they were reckoned while the actual operations were still in progress, and at a time when we still had no access to the relevant enemy records. Moreover, in the case of damaged vessels in particular, precise confirmation of individual successes is very difficult to get. In general these figures do, however, give a reasonable indication of the results achieved. These results are further borne out by a separate post-war investigation into *sinkings only* of German coastwise shipping (including certain minor naval units) between September, 1939, and January, 1945, in the coastal and enclosed waters from the North Cape to the Spanish frontier in the Bay of Biscay—an investigation which attributed 22·7 per cent. of the 920 sinkings to surface ships and submarines, and the remaining 77·3 per cent. to aircraft attack and mines (most of which were laid from the air). It is of interest to note that the major contribution was made by mining in the Kattegat, Great Belt and Baltic, by Bomber Command—the small cloud had grown ! It is also as well to remember, in assessing the effect of this blockade, that the loss of trade due to delays caused by the blockade was about twice the loss due directly to sinkings.

When, at the end of May, 1940, the German

Army and the Luftwaffe had pinned the British Expeditionary Force and a fragment of the French Army up against the coast round Dunkirk, there appeared no choice but surrender or annihilation. The enemy forces, land and air, were at the height of their power, and flushed with victory. Air superiority had throughout been one of the keynotes of the German success. It is true we had superior naval forces, but they were mainly in Scottish waters, and Norway had shown that they could not hope to operate freely, or without risk of serious loss, in face of enemy air superiority. History has recorded few, if any, situations which appeared more hopeless. Yet, compounded out of the stubborn courage of the B.E.F., the gallantry and discipline of the Royal Navy, and of the crews of that fantastic amateur fleet which emerged from the rivers and seaside resorts, and out of the determined air offensive by the aircrews who were all too few in number, finally there emerged the " Miracle of Dunkirk." In eight days 316,663 troops were evacuated from Dunkirk and those crowded beaches. The pilots and aircrews of Fighter Command, Bomber Command, Coastal Command, and the Fleet Air Arm during those critical days established a moral ascendancy over the enemy which did much to outweigh the enemy's numerical advantage, and, fighting to a large extent out of sight behind the enemy lines, they saved the beaches from becoming a shambles. As Mr. Churchill said in his statement in Parliament on 5th June : " Wars are not won by evacuations.

But there was a victory inside this deliverance which should be noted. It was gained by the Air Force." Sea power had extracted the Allied forces from the clutches of the victorious German Army and Air Force—sea power exercised by a motley fleet of destroyers, passenger vessels, motor boats and yachts, under cover of an air force which owed its strength to training and morale and not its numbers.

Three years later at Tunis a similar situation arose ; but the boot was on the other foot. This time the defeated Army was German and Italian. It, too, wished to get home, and it, too, had to cross the sea to escape. There also the victorious side had air superiority. But there the analogy breaks down. Long before the final battle of Tunis was over on the ground, the Allied Air Forces had begun to spread the tentacles of air superiority across the Sicilian Straits, over the Sicilian airfields and ports. Seaborne supply of the Armies in Tunisia had become almost impossible by April ; evacuation by sea, except for a few handfuls by destroyer, became hopeless. Finally, even destroyers came to grief and there were desperate attempts to evacuate by air. The final stages became to the Allied Forces almost like a rat hunt. During April alone some 200 enemy air transports were destroyed, the peak being the destruction in one engagement of eighteen out of twenty M.E.323s (a large four-engined glider type with a ten-ton payload). The battle of Tunis was won by 7th May. On the

9th, daylight patrols by Allied destroyers were established to cut off any strays. 248,000 German and Italian prisoners, including von Arnim and his staff, were captured. Only a handful escaped before the final closure. Here, in this climax of the African campaigns, was air power denying the sea to the enemy.

This, however, was only the climax, and I want to go back to the early days of the Mediterranean Campaign and briefly trace the vicissitudes of sea, air, and land power from Taranto to Tunis. The Mediterranean Campaign as a whole would well repay careful study. Operations were on a smaller scale than the mass campaigns on the Continent of Europe; but, excepting the " V " and atomic weapons, every aspect and form of modern war was exemplified, and the interplay of land, sea and air warfare can clearly be seen throughout.

In the latter part of 1940 the British fleet in the Mediterranean, though numerically inferior to the Italian both in overall strength and in capital ships, had established—morally at any rate—command at sea in most parts of the Mediterranean. Admiral Cunningham spent most of his time trailing his coat in the vain hope of drawing the Italian fleet into action. In July he had had an engagement which the Italians broke off, much to his disappointment. Italian bombers carried out a series of attacks on the British fleet without real effect. " But " said Admiral Cunningham in his report, " the action was not without value. It must have shown the Italians that their Air Force

and their submarines cannot stop our fleet pene-
trating into the central Mediterranean, and that
only their main fleet can seriously interfere with
our operating there." On that well-proven basis
the British fleet continued to trail its coat, the
aircraft carriers *Illustrious* and *Hermes* entered the
Ægean to bombard Leros, and on 11th November
aircraft from the *Illustrious* carried out a highly
successful attack on the Italian fleet at Taranto
Harbour, which crippled three battleships and
two cruisers. During the following month the
fleet was active also in carrying out bombardments at various points on the Mediterranean
coasts. All this was in keeping with the finest
traditions of the past—but what had been true
of the Italian was not necessarily true of the
German.

Towards the end of the year the Luftwaffe had
begun to operate in the Mediterranean theatre,
and the first attempt to reduce Malta to impotence
as a naval and air base had begun. Early in
January, while covering an eastbound convoy
into Malta, the aircraft carrier *Illustrious* was
severely damaged by a heavy German air attack.
Though crippled and on fire, the ship was got
into Malta. While lying there she was further
damaged, but it was finally found possible to sail
her successfully to Alexandria. In the meantime
the cruiser *Gloucester* had been damaged, and the
Southampton sunk by air attack en route to
Alexandria. Times had begun to change.

In March we had become committed to send a

land force to support the Greeks against the German threat, and the British Navy had had a heavy commitment in covering convoys into the Ægean to Greece. No transports were lost, though two cruisers were lost to submarines. Then on 28th March came the last main fleet engagement in the Mediterranean, the Battle of Cape Matapan. Air attacks on the Italian Fleet by carrier-borne and shore-based aircraft opened the battle, causing early damage to the battleship *Vittorio Veneto*, and later crippling one of the Italian cruisers in the evening. Though the battleship's speed was reduced, this was not sufficient to enable the British Fleet to overtake her. The cruiser, on the other hand, was brought to a dead stop, which was what probably determined the subsequent movements of the Italian Fleet and gave Admiral Cunningham his opportunity of engaging—with the added advantage that this could be done at night, when there was virtually no danger from enemy aircraft. This proved to be a thoroughly efficient and highly successful operation : one Italian battleship damaged, three new cruisers and two new destroyers sunk ; all for no British ships lost. Coming on top of the successful air attack at Taranto, this operation, by drastically altering in our favour the balance of naval strength, would, under the conditions of sea warfare as we used to know them, have confirmed British command at sea in the Mediterranean for an indefinite period. Moreover, the British fleet's bombardment of Tripoli a few weeks later apparently underlined that verdict. Times, however, changed. The experience of the *Illustrious* was only one of a number of straws showing which way the wind was blowing. Ever since the Desert campaign opened, the Navy had given invaluable support by running supplies along the coast to supplement the meagre land line of communications ; they had also at times carried out coastal bombardments. Gradually, however, after the arrival of the Germans these operations became more and more expensive. When, during the first retreat, the garrison of Tobruk was left isolated, a heavy additional burden was placed on the Mediterranean and on the Navy. Tobruk depended for its life on seaborne supplies, was out of effective range of our nearest fighter airstrips, and the perimeter was so small that it was quite impossible to maintain any fighters on the spot. Seaborne supplies were run up as far as possible under cover of a fighter escort, but the last part of the run and the turn round in Tobruk had to be done without direct protection against air attack other than that provided by A.A. Though local air superiority over Tobruk was not possible, the Desert Air Force were able to establish and maintain general air superiority over the Axis air forces, the enemy were never strong enough to attempt a knockout blow at Tobruk at that time, and the seaborne supplies were maintained, though at a heavy cost—mostly caused by enemy submarines.

On 6th April, 1941, the German invasion of Greece began. On 24th April, overwhelmed on land and in the air, the British forces began their evacuation from Greece. It is perhaps worth noting here that a successful German air attack on shipping at Piræus, which led to the explosion of an ammunition ship in harbour, had a critical effect on the supplies for the British Army and a demoralising effect on the Greeks, out of all proportion to the material damage. The small British Air Force had sacrificed itself almost completely during the brief and hopeless campaign, and by the time the evacuation began there were no aircraft left to cover the beaches, and barely two dozen aircraft left with which to challenge the enemy's air superiority over the sea approaches. They did all they could and more ; from Crete a number of attacks on our transports were intercepted and diverted, but the losses of ships and men were heavy : all one can say is that they would have been heavier still but for that devoted handful of airmen. Nevertheless, the great bulk of the British troops were safely evacuated—over 50,000 officers and men.

I have in a previous lecture spoken of the enemy air superiority over Crete ; the invasion of Crete was, in fact, air power exercised in its most simple form, and based entirely on air superiority. At this point, however, I want to examine the effect of that air superiority and air power on the exercise of sea power. During the interval between our evacuation and the opening of the attack on Crete, attempts were made to send supplies and equipment to our forces in Crete to replace their losses.

Of 27,000 tons despatched to Crete by sea, 21,000 tons were turned back to Egypt, and 3,400 tons were lost at sea due to air action. Less than 3,000 tons reached Crete. The actual invasion of Crete was somewhat of an improvisation. The Germans had had the training, and they had the equipment for the air invasion, but they had not the equipment or special shipping for a follow-up by sea and consequently had to improvise with local caiques and other small craft. The same day as the air invasion of Crete began, 20th May, our air reconnaissance had located one or two collections of caiques in the islands, evidently organised in some form or another. Three British naval squadrons were disposed in Cretan waters, with a view to meeting the possibility of a seaborne invasion. On the evening of the 21st one of these squadrons intercepted a convoy of caiques, sank one escorting destroyer, and sank or set on fire the caiques, with a loss to the enemy of some three or four thousand men. During that day we had one cruiser damaged and one destroyer sunk by air attack. The following day one of our other squadrons sighted another convoy of caiques in the Ægean, north of Crete. The convoy was dispersed, but the squadron, being under very heavy attack, turned away. During this operation two of our cruisers were heavily damaged by air attack. The same day, in the waters around Crete, we suffered two cruisers and a destroyer sunk and two battleships damaged.

By this time it was necessary for the fleet to

re-fuel—Suda Bay, which had been the advanced base, now, of course, being unusable. Two more destroyers were lost to air attack during the withdrawal to Alexandria. While the battle in Crete was being fought out the naval C.-in-C. decided that the best way he could help the Army in Crete was by trying to reduce the enemy's air effort by attacking one of their airfields—that on the island of Scarpanto. A successful attack was carried out on the 25th by carrier-borne aircraft, but during the withdrawal the carrier H.M.S. *Formidable*, newly arrived in the Mediterranean, was badly damaged by air attack, as also was one of the escorting destroyers. Two days later the British Government ordered the evacuation of Crete. The first evacuation had to be from Heraclion on the north side of the island, the others from a point on the south coast south of Canea. There were few aircraft available in Egypt and the Desert which had the range and the performance to give effective cover to these convoys : a carefully timed programme was, however, arranged so as to make the most use of the hours of darkness for the actual embarkation and passage close to Crete—the Luftwaffe had shown itself surprisingly ineffective at night. The four convoys from South Crete were on the whole successfully covered, the only casualty being one cruiser damaged and a number of air attacks being driven off. The evacuation from Heraclion was less successful : a cruiser and destroyer were severely damaged on the way north, and on the way out the convoy was seriously delayed in departure by a defect on one of the ships ; they were unable to make their rendezvous with the air escort, and unable to give their position. They were heavily attacked by air throughout much of the homeward passage ; two more destroyers were sunk and a cruiser very badly damaged—the latter with very heavy casualties—and another cruiser and destroyer hit. The final casualty was another cruiser sunk north of Alexandria : she was sent out to assist the last of the Crete convoys, and as she was specially equipped as an A.A. ship no arrangements were made for air cover. Over 17,000 troops were evacuated from Crete. The price in surface ships was three cruisers and six destroyers sunk ; one battleship, one aircraft carrier, three cruisers and one destroyer seriously damaged ; and one battleship, four cruisers and six destroyers in need of extensive repairs. Against these material losses there was on the credit side a record of wonderful gallantry and determination.

Once again, magnificent, but not war. To operate surface ships, as we then had to, inside a circle of enemy air bases, under an enemy air superiority which, for lack of aircraft and bases, was unchallengeable—this was clearly no longer an operation of war. Conditions had changed. The forces we had been trying to operate in the Balkans and Eastern Mediterranean were clearly out of balance. We had had the sea forces, but with the air forces and air bases to secure air superiority lacking, the ability to retain command at sea was clearly slipping from our hands. Command at sea in the Ægean had in fact passed to the German Air Force, and was in danger of passing to them in the Mediterranean itself.

I want to digress here for a moment or two to say a few words about airborne operations. The capture of Crete was an example of the exercise of air power, air power overriding sea power ; sea power was virtually helpless. The question arises—and it is one of utmost importance to the security of Britain—whether the possibilities of airborne invasion vitiate sea power as one of the main pillars of our security ? During the European War, while no major operation was carried out by the Germans after Crete, the Allies carried out four such operations—two across intervening sea and two across major rivers. Three of them were in varying degrees successful. The other, though initially successful, failed in its ultimate object. In each case the object was, by using the air approach coupled with surprise, to bridge the gap while the main forces on land were overcoming the inevitable handicap of the water-borne approach. There are, I think, certain characteristics of airborne operations which it is important to appreciate. In the first place, an airborne force is extremely vulnerable while in the air, both to enemy air and to ground defences. Without complete local air superiority it is literally not feasible. A.A. defences may make the losses prohibitive. During the invasion of Crete the Germans, as we have seen, had complete local air superiority, but their losses, due in a large measure to the meagre A.A. defences, were so heavy that there was a period when the whole attempt was all but abandoned. In the second place it must be remembered that an airborne force, once landed, is, sooner rather then later, dependent on normal supply and support by land and sea. One of the reasons for the partial failure of the Arnhem operation was the inability of the supporting forces to fight their way through to join up in time ; and the heavy air losses in the final stage were due to attempts to re-supply by air after the initial surprise had passed away. In short, so far as the security of these islands is concerned, sea power under cover of air power still has its place ; the great bulk of any attempted invasion must still come by sea. Finally, there is the question as to what is involved in the staging of an airborne operation on the scale used during the late war. I use the word " staging " deliberately. It is an extremely complicated business involving highly specialised training and equipment, both air and ground. How complex is the staging of the final operation is indicated by the fact that before Arnhem no less than fifteen airborne operations were successively planned and preparations started, which had, one after the other, to be shelved because they could not be got ready in time—events on the ground had moved too fast. During most of that time the bulk of the air transport force was immobilised preparing for operations which never came off.

In the Normandy landings nearly 1,500 transport aircraft and 860 gliders were employed. At Arnhem the numbers were greater still; no less than 2,500 gliders were employed. Each one of these airborne attacks made great contributions to the success of our overall strategy, but when one remembers what they involved in the aircraft, special material and training needed in order to cross the water—in order to side-step sea power by using air power—one gets a useful reminder of the fact that the sea is still a very real factor in security. We must also heed the warning that though such operations can be staged in the days of plenty, the question to what extent it is possible or wise in peacetime to devote the limited available effort to this highly specialised and limited field is one that calls for very careful consideration.

But to return to the Mediterranean. Throughout the whole of the Mediterranean campaign from 1940 till mid-1943 there was one dominating theme, the ultimate aim the whole time was the same—to secure freedom to use the sea routes through and across the Mediterranean. We and the enemy both had the same ultimate aim, but our outlooks on the problem were not the same. The Axis requirement was to be able to use the sea routes across to Africa so as to supply the armies which alone could finish the job by clearing us out of Egypt. Our requirement was to keep the route open from Gibraltar, through Malta, to Egypt. It is true we had alternative routes, expensive though they were : the sea route via the Cape and the air route via Takoradi on the west coast of Africa. The Axis problem was simpler than ours, since the sea routes they needed to Tripoli and Benghazi were far shorter than ours, and far less exposed to attack—except from Malta. Our problem was difficult, because we only held points at each end of the 1,700 mile route and one point—Malta—at the centre. The key to our position in the whole Mediterranean lay in Malta. Thanks to the Cape and Takoradi routes, the forces in Egypt could at a price manage reasonably without the use of the Mediterranean route ; but the retention of Malta was literally vital, not only to any possibility of denying the cross-sea route to the enemy, but also to any prospects of re-opening the through route.

As an offensive base from which to operate naval and air forces against the enemy supply routes Malta was ideal. It was central. All the main ports of departure and arrival were within range of air reconnaissance ; from Malta, surface naval ships could operate under cover of darkness over a wide radius ; bomber and torpedo aircraft based on Malta could only be evaded by wide divergencies off the direct routes ; for submarines also it was an ideally situated base. But two dangers threatened it : firstly, direct destruction of the base itself by air attack, and, secondly, starving out the islands by cessation of supply. Three times, when the use of Malta as an offensive base seriously threatened the maintenance of the Axis effort in Africa, did the German try to neutralise it by direct attack : early in 1941, again during the first quarter of 1942, and finally in the summer. Three times he failed to get that ultimate degree of air superiority which would have enabled him to deliver the *coup-de-grâce*. During 1941 the Axis failed to prevent the passage of adequate supplies to Malta both from the east and west. We suffered losses, especially in the naval escort, but the supplies got through. During that period, on the other hand, we were able to make very effective use of Malta. In the six months from May to October, 1941, over 270,000 tons of Axis shipping was sunk on the African convoy routes, of which 47 per cent. was sunk by air action and 44 per cent. by submarine. According to a German source, the percentage of African supplies sunk or damaged by all causes varied from 16 per cent. in July to 77 per cent. in November, 1941 (*see Diagram No. 3*). It is important to remember in this connection that some of Rommel's losses resulted from attacks on Naples, Palermo and Taranto, Tripoli and Benghazi.

But Rommel had already become aware of the danger by August, 1941, and in October the neutralisation of Malta was ordered by Hitler and Mussolini. The Axis air forces accordingly began assembling in Sicily in November, and the British advance in the desert which immediately followed lent an added spur to the enemy's drastic intentions—for it was now even more essential than ever to reinforce Rommel and build up his

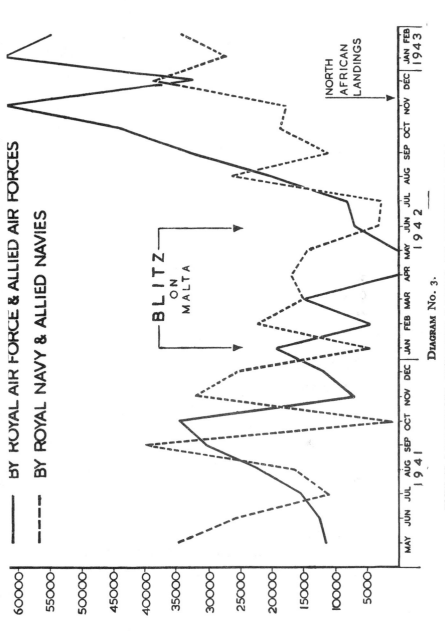

DIAGRAM No. 3.

ENEMY MERCHANT SHIPPING LOSSES IN MEDITERRANEAN

supplies. The weight of attack on Malta was multiplied by ten in December, doubled again in January, and quadrupled in March. The few surface ships which had come to assist Malta's defence in November, 1941, had now to be withdrawn again to Alexandria. In April more than 6,000 tons fell on the island and Malta was on her knees. In May further Spitfire reinforcements were flown in from Allied carriers (including U.S.S. *Wasp*) and the tide turned. But in the interval Rommel had got some supplies (not, indeed, all that he wanted, but he was fortunate in that the next phase of the land battle enabled him to recoup himself handsomely from captured material), and our Desert offensive was turned into a retreat, which but for our air superiority might well have been a rout, and which only stopped at Alamein.

The danger then was twofold ; both Egypt and Malta were in jeopardy—Egypt from direct invasion and Malta from starvation. The loss of the airfields in Cyrenaica made effective cover of the Malta convoys impossible. Even in January the loss of the airfields at Benghazi and in the ' Bulge " had made the passage of convoys precarious in the extreme. One attempt in February had only resulted in total loss, and a second attempt in March, supported by action on land, at sea, and in the air, lost only one of four ships at sea, skilfully evaded the main Italian fleet which came out to intercept, and reached Malta, only to be destroyed in harbour with loss of most of the precious stores. In June a further and more ambitious attempt was made to get supplies through to Malta. Two convoys were to run through simultaneously from east and west. Of seventeen merchant ships in the two convoys, only two from the east-bound convoy reached Malta. We lost two cruisers and five destroyers and others damaged : the enemy lost one cruiser to air and submarine attack. This took place during the critical phase of the land battle, and by the time the abortive west-bound convoy arrived back at Alexandria our forces in the Desert were in full retreat. With our air forces back behind Alamein any possibility of getting a west-bound convoy through had gone. Meanwhile, Malta's situation as regards both military supplies and food daily became more critical. One convoy of fourteen ships had, indeed, been despatched from Gibraltar in August. But despite a heavy escort, including three aircraft carriers and two battleships, and despite every effort by the Malta-based fighters as soon as the convoy came within range, only five ships of the convoy were able to reach harbour. The remainder were sunk by enemy air action—as also was the *Eagle*, while the *Indomitable* suffered damage. This gallant convoy did, indeed, afford valuable relief to the island, but on nothing like the scale required. Malta had surmounted her second and third blitzes, and for months, short of all supplies though she was, had come again as the centre from which Rommel's supply line was being strangled ; and now, when she was starving, her value as a base was more important than ever.

Thanks largely to the Malta-based attacks, Rommel also was starving, especially for oil. The question was : would the 8th Army be ready in time—before sufficient supplies had evaded our blockade to set Rommel on his feet again ; and would it be able to drive him back beyond Benghazi in time, so that we could re-establish our air forces in the Bulge and thus get convoys through to Malta before it was too late ? It was a fine-drawn affair, and there were anxious days, even after the Battle of Alamein had at last started but moved slowly. The story goes that Rommel saw the last of his tankers sunk by our torpedo aircraft before his eyes at the entrance to Tobruk harbour. Our Air Force airfield parties went forward with our leading troops—sometimes getting ahead of them. The day they reached Tobruk the convoy for Malta sailed from Alexandria, and when it passed the Bulge the following day our fighters were operating from airfields in the Bulge. The convoy got through untouched, and Malta was saved. During that last quarter, from August to November, 1942, 205,000 tons of Axis shipping was sunk, 35 per cent. by submarine, 61 per cent. by air action (*see Diagram No.* 3). A German source gives Rommel's losses as 59 per cent. in October, of which two-thirds was petrol. Five tankers in succession were sunk. I have already referred to the final climax at Tunis, but even in these relatively early days the enemy saw the red light. The day after the North Africa landings the Reichskommissar for shipping reported: "Field-Marshal General Rommel informed me of his opinion on the devastating situation of sea transport in the Mediterranean, where things are in a complete mess." Three weeks later the German Naval C.-in-C. repeated previous complaints, saying : " It was especially pointed out what consequences would ensue for the continuance of sea transport to Tunisia, and above all to Tripolitania, if, with the constant strengthening of the enemy in Malta and Algiers, we did not succeed in securing German air superiority in the central Mediterranean." The situation was summed up by the Commander of the Afrika Corps : " Alamein was lost before it was fought, we had not the petrol. Vast stocks of petrol and material were lying around in Italy and the Italians were supposed to bring them over, but they were unable to do it."

The land campaign in the Desert had in fact been, and continued to be, a fight for air bases ; air bases from which we could stretch forward our air superiority over the enemy's ports and sea supply routes, superiority under cover of which our air forces and naval forces, surface and submarine, could secure command at sea—deny the sea routes to the enemy and secure them for ourselves. The new North Africa campaign fitted into the same pattern, a pattern in which land, sea and air power are closely interwoven, but of which the key is air superiority.

So far I have discussed examples of air power during the late war in which its entity as part of a trinity can be most clearly seen ; but before I close this lecture I want briefly to consider air power in relation to sea power in circumstances where land operations were not so directly affected. It was in the Pacific that air power came into view most dramatically as a vital and perhaps the dominant factor in command at sea. The treacherous blow by which Japanese carrier-borne aircraft upset the balance of naval power in the Pacific, crippling five U.S. battleships in one surprise attack, set the pace from the outset. The basic problem was the same as in the West—air superiority and air bases—but in view of the enormous distances between existing or potential land-air bases, coupled with the limited range of aircraft at that time, the initial air bases had to be floating ones, and the fight for air superiority became a fight to destroy the opposing aircraft carriers. The two decisive battles, the battle of the Coral Sea, which turned the tide in Australian waters, and the Battle of Midway, which opened the road for the counter-offensive into Japanese waters, were both air battles fought out far beyond range of the surface ships' guns. They cost the Japanese six of their fleet carriers, and the Americans two. In the Pacific, two campaigns were fought concurrently : one step by step westward across the Pacific, from carrier-air base to island air-base, and then again from carrier air-base to island air-base ; the other northward from shore base to shore base back to the Philippines, where the two combined forces joined at Leyte and the Japanese surface and seaborne air forces suffered the knockout blow in a desperate and confused battle in which it is almost impossible to differentiate between the results achieved by air, surface and submarine action. Whether the immense effort involved by the seaborne air force was actually the most economical method of solving the difficult problem of great ocean distances I cannot say. That it was effective there can be no doubt, and it culminated in the establishment of the air bases in the Marianas, Iwojima, and on Okinawa from which the final and decisive air attacks were delivered. It is difficult, however, to overlook the fact that the performance, especially in hitting power, of land-based aircraft is inevitably far greater than that of ship-borne aircraft, and, moreover, that aircraft carriers are not like Malta—unsinkable. One cannot help wondering what would have happened had the Japanese adopted earlier on the suicide tactics which at Okinawa sank scores of ships. Moreover, I think one must remember that the Pacific, with its huge ocean spaces, is a special case. Even before the end of the late war shore-based aircraft were operating over the mid-Atlantic and beyond.

I think it is interesting to compare the Japanese problem with our own. Japan, like Britain, depended for her very existence on the ability to maintain her seaborne supplies. Once she had, by her widespread initial successes, created an

" Empire," she, like Britain, depended for the maintenance of that " Empire " on command at sea, on her ability to maintain the flow of seaborne supplies to her occupying forces. Like Britain, Japan had two main threats to meet : attacks on her shipping and air attack on her home base, possibly leading in the end to invasion ; but, as she was the aggressor, Japan's problems arose in the opposite order to that in which Britain had to face her problems. The Battle of Britain was at the beginning of Britain's war, the battle of Japan was at the end of hers. Japan gradually lost control of the sea routes as Britain gradually regained them. In our struggle against the U-boats, as technique developed and the available air and surface escort strength increased, the danger area was gradually pushed farther and farther from our shores, the enemy's endeavour being to operate out of range of our aircraft and escort vessels. It was a long-drawn-out campaign with its difficult times : when we found the U-boats were faster on the surface than our escort vessels, when they began to hunt in packs, when they found us unprepared in the Caribbean and sank more than a million of tanker tonnage, when they mounted heavy A.A. armament and fought it out with our aircraft, when they produced the Schnorkel, which enabled them to charge batteries submerged ; but each move was met by technique and tactics, and though the defeat of the U-boat was essentially a combined operation by air and sea forces, more and more did aircraft come to be the dominant factor in the campaign.

The Japanese, on the other hand, failed to appreciate the vital importance of the air as a part of the defence against submarine attack. The American campaign against the Japanese supplies was a complex pattern ; as the U.S. Bombing Survey reports puts it : " Long-range air search found targets for the submarines ; convoying, which offered some protection against submarines, increased the vulnerability to air attack ; ships driven into congested harbours in fear of submarines were an easy prey for carrier strikes ; and mines helped to drive ships out of shallow waters into waters where submarines could operate." The key to the pattern from the Japanese point of view was, as it was in the Atlantic and Mediterranean, air power. Fortunately they appear to have completely failed to realize that the air superiority which they provided for in their initial attacks was a continuing problem, that the fight for it never stops. As with the Germans, so with the Japanese, they used up their skilled and experienced air personnel at the outset, and did not, until too late, begin to provide for training of the men and production of the aircraft needed to maintain the continuous air war. Nearly nine million tons out of a total available of just over ten million tons of Japanese shipping was out of action at the end of the war, either sunk or seriously damaged ; nearly 55 per cent. of this was attributable to submarines, and some 40 per cent. to air attack of different kinds. After April, 1945, 50 per cent. of all ships sunk or damaged were victims of mines dropped by B.29s—an interesting comparison with Bomber Command's results against German shipping.

Finally, a brief word about air power on the more conventional plane. One of the standard principles in naval strategy has been what is called the " fleet in being "—the fact that all sea movements in a given area are affected by the mere presence of a strong naval force in that area, and that that influence persists so long as that force is present as a potential threat, even though it may never be engaged. There is no similar war-time principle applicable to air forces. As I have already pointed out, an air force order of battle is by itself no firm criterion of its true strength, since there are many imponderable factors which only show themselves in action ; an air force can only be judged when put to the test of action, and consequently it is unlikely to be taken at its face value if it remains inactive ; in war-time an " air force in being " is not likely to be a power in the land. On the other hand, the tonnage, armour, speed, and armament of naval ships are positive and calculable factors which can be decisive in action, and there is no doubt that the " fleet in being " continued during the late war to have a great influence on strategy and on operations at sea and in the air. In this game the most powerful ships have so far held the trumps. Although no fleet action took place, the mere

presence in German waters of a fleet, small in
numbers though it was, involved us in a continuous commitment as regards the maintenance,
development and dispositions of our own fleet.
It involved a considerable commitment for our air
forces as well—frequent reconnaissance to locate
the whereabouts of the main German units, air
striking forces at readiness, and extensive air
defences for our fleet bases. In the Pacific war,
although most of the actions were between carrier-
borne aircraft and ships and not directly ship to
ship, the existence of a Japanese battle fleet led
to the creation of a bigger and better American
battle fleet, which held the ring while the carriers
operated. It was, however, aircraft and submarines that claimed most of the big ship victims
on both sides during the war and the inevitable
questions are being asked—Does the big ship
principle still apply under modern conditions?
Have aircraft and submarines defeated the unsinkable battleship of which we were told before
the war? Is the " fleet in being " theory tenable
in face of air attack? These are difficult questions
to answer when one remembers our experience off
Singapore, the sinking of at least one latest
Japanese battleship by aircraft off Leyte; still
more difficult when one remembers the capital
ships which came to ignominious ends in harbour.
These are not questions to be lightly answered in
either sense. Big issues are involved and calm,
unprejudiced judgment is needed. The facts of
the late war need very careful and impartial

analysis, and the possibilities of the future need skilled and scientific assessment. All I would venture to say on this issue is that we cannot afford to make the wrong decision ; we are unlikely again to be given time to correct a mistake ; we must be ready for the future, not the past

— 4 —

THE EXERCISE OF AIR POWER

THERE have been some enthusiasts who have stated that air power can by itself win wars. As regards the late war it is clear that we did not attempt to win by means of air power alone—or even by air power as the primary factor. It is true that in the autumn of 1940, and again in March, 1941, aircraft production was given, by the Cabinet, the highest possible priority with the especial object of building up Bomber Command to the greatest possible strength. In practice, however, the distribution of the national war effort did not work out like that. As regards man-power within the Services, the Army in 1939 had about six times and in 1944 three times the strength of the Air Force. Of the direct war effort of the nation the Army accounted for about half, the Air Force just over and the Navy just under a quarter. Civil Defence absorbed about 3 per cent. The bomber force itself, taking into account the man-power cost of production, maintenance and training, and also of the actual bomb loads dropped, took approximately 12 per cent. at the peak, and, over the whole war, 7 per cent.

of the direct war effort of the nation. Seven per cent. Moreover, in considering that figure one must remember that the bomber force, even more perhaps than the Navy, was fully engaged in operations throughout the war, whereas for some four years only a part of the Army was fully engaged, and the Army as a whole was therefore not making such heavy demands as it would otherwise have done. No, whatever some enthusiasts may have claimed as possible, in practice we did not try to use the air as the real war-winner. Whether in fact it did ultimately show the potentialities of a war-winner I will leave you to judge when I have finished this lecture. I doubt, however, whether one derives much value from arguments as to whether or not one arm or other of the defence forces can win wars single-handed : in my view all three arms of defence are inevitably involved, though the correct balance between them may and will vary. What we must, however, get clear in our minds is the answer to the question, how much air power by itself can contribute towards winning a war ; and what is more there must be no finality to that answer—it must be continually adjusted to keep pace with the developments which science and technology bring. Without an answer to that question we cannot hope to arrive at and maintain a proper balance between the various arms of our national defence.

It is not an easy question to answer on the evidence of the late war since air operations on both sides were so closely, though to a varying extent, linked with operations on land and at sea. Owing to the extreme flexibility of air striking power, it came, during the late war, to be employed for such a great variety of tasks that it is almost impossible to differentiate between what was and what was not designed to support some other operations. The flexibility of air force is indeed one of its dominant characteristics. From one base area it can strike at a variety of targets over a wide area; conversely, from widely separated bases it can strike at a single target or target system. By " target system " I mean a number of targets all related to a single object: for example, where the object was to counter the U-boat attack, targets would include U-boat bases, U-boat shipbuilding yards, factories where components such as Diesel engines were made; where the object was to reduce the enemy air effort, the target system included airfields, airframe factories, aero-engine factories, component factories, radio factories. Given centralised control of air forces, this flexibility brings with it an immense power of concentration which is unequalled in any other form of warfare. In other words, if properly used, the flexibility of air force enables it to be highly economical.

The important words in my previous sentences are " if properly used " and " given centralised control." It has been interesting to note how the general attitude towards the air striking force— the bombers—alters with circumstances. Before the late war there was a fairly common tendency to regard the bomber as a somewhat improper weapon and an extravagance quite unnecessary for defence. Then in the early stages of the war there arose a demand for " dive bombers " on the German model. When the dive bomber was debunked by our fighters, or even before that, it began to be realised in many quarters that the bomber could do many things regarded as essential which were otherwise impossible. Many were the authorities who found " essential " jobs for the bomber force to carry out. The experts on economic war thought out one class of industrial target after another, the destruction of which would, they argued, cripple the enemy's war effort —synthetic oil plants, synthetic rubber factories, molybdenum mines, hydro-electric plants, ball-bearing factories, optical works, aluminium plants, motor assembly plants, coke ovens, iron and steel plants, industrial towns, etc. The experts in maritime war called for attacks on the enemy ships in harbour (the " fleet in being "), on U-boat bases including towns where U-boat crews rested, and on shipbuilding yards. The experts in land warfare called for attacks on tank factories, on fuel dumps, on ordnance depots, on fixed defences, on towns (to cause road blocks), on troop concentrations, on headquarters, and on bridges (to sever communications). They also found great advantages in a process which came to be known as " softening up " : air operations in which the maximum number of heavy bombers dropped the maximum weight of high explosive in the minimum time on a limited area facing the line of assault—a concentration in time, space, and weight of explosive far greater than that obtainable in any other way. The expert in air warfare also had his own target system as part of his campaign for air superiority—enemy airfields, radar warning stations, aircraft, and aero-engine factories. Those who were concerned in Home Defence would press for attacks on " V " weapon experimental stations, " V " weapon factories, launching sites, storage sites, oxygen plants, and hydrogen peroxide plants. It is perhaps not the first time that the Cinderella has come to be the maid of all work. Nearly everyone had vital jobs for the bombers. In fact there were so many cooks who wanted to stir the bombers' broth that, had there been no centralised control, no head cook with a firm hand, there would have been a very real danger of flexibility in itself resulting not in concentration and economy of effort, but in dispersal and waste of effort.

Air warfare cannot be separated into little packets ; it knows no boundaries on land or sea other than those imposed by the radius of action of the aircraft ; it is a unity and demands unity of command. In the Middle East campaign we were fortunate in that all the air forces—day and night fighters, fighter bombers and long-range fighters, day and night bombers, reconnaissance over land and sea, torpedo bombers—all came under one centralised command, and it was possible to switch and concentrate against the vital target as the day-by-day situation changed. It was possible for torpedo aircraft from Malta, fighters from the Desert, and long-range bombers from Egypt, to concentrate in time and space : on one occasion, during the height of a land battle, they did so to such a tune that the British torpedo aircraft from the Desert en route to Malta, and American bombers from the Canal Zone attacked the Italian fleet almost simultaneously, three hours after Malta-based torpedo aircraft had crippled an Italian cruiser which incidentally received its *coup de grace* from a submarine an hour later.

In Britain the problem of centralised control was more difficult than in the Mediterranean theatre. In the first place it is important to remember that for some four years after the evacuation of Dunkirk the bomber offensive was the only means of attacking Germany. The Mediterranean campaigns were invaluable in bleeding Germany of some of her best man-power and material, but, until their final stages, they were in essence defensive. For all those years, apart from the bomber offensive, we could do no more than nibble at the fringes of German occupied territory. It was, therefore, inevitable that the Government itself should take a close interest in the bomber operations. There were also phases of the war when the bomber operations were an important factor in the war at sea, and, later on, in the defence against the so-called " V " weapons, a fact which on more than one occasion led to direct intervention by the Government in the allocation of the bomber effort. The Ministry of Economic Warfare was concerned in advising on industrial and economic targets, the Ministry of Home Security advised on the interpretation of photo cover of bombed German targets, a committee of oil specialists advised on oil targets, and there were also joint committees representing all three Services : when the American air force came they had corresponding intelligence committees which linked in with the British ones. Finally there were the Chiefs of Staff who directed the operations on land, at sea, and in the air. It was the Chief of the Air Staff who, except during the Normandy campaign, directed the bomber offensive, first on behalf of the Chiefs of Staff, and, in the final stage, in co-operation with the Commanding General of the United States Army Air Forces, on behalf of the Combined Chiefs of Staff. I give all this detail because in some quarters I think the idea existed that the Air Forces were always going off fighting a private war of their own. If there had been such a tendency there were ample safeguards against it.

Nevertheless, there are air operations which can be undertaken without being directly related to operations on land or at sea. Such operations have a political or economic objective. The simplest example of this use of air power is the operations that have been carried out on the North-West Frontier of India. There was a case in the latter part of 1946 when one of the frontier tribes kidnapped a British political agent. The

Indian Government decided to assert their authority, and when the tribe ignored their summons they decided to show force. After warning leaflets had been dropped, which still failed to bring the tribe to terms (though they did in consequence evacuate their villages) air action was taken as a result of which the tribe complied with the Government's terms. Strangely enough, operations of this sort are singularly economical in lives as well as in effort. That indeed is one of the main reasons why they have been developed. In the particular case I have just quoted there were in fact no columns of troops involved, no outposts, no fighting. The total casualties on both sides were seven, of which six were accidental. Had this operation been undertaken on the ground, it was estimated that three brigade groups of troops would have been required for about two months, together with suitable air support and air supply ; this might have involved a large-scale tribal insurrection. In dealing with a very similar frontier problem in 1936–37, forces of varying size, which finally amounted to two divisional headquarters and five infantry brigades with supporting cavalry and artillery, were employed for some six months ; our own casualties then numbered 164 killed and 431 wounded, and those of the tribesmen 715 killed and 657 wounded.

The German attempt to use air by itself was very different. It was not a considered operation. In 1940 they gave up the military object of neutralising the R.A.F. preparatory to invasion, and passed to the political one of forcing surrender by destroying London and thus breaking the morale of the British people. It was a method which had succeeded in Poland and Holland, and in Denmark the threat of such action had sufficed. The change took place, as we have seen, because they had failed in their first plan. The second failed because the population of London was tough, because the enemy did not persevere, because they had to divert many of their resources to their new campaign against Russia, but also because they were beaten in the air—they never attained effective air superiority. Whether such air attack would have failed if they had had air forces comparable with those employed by the Anglo–American forces in 1944, and had operated such forces to a definite plan, is a moot point. The final attacks on London in 1944, by bombers and the " V " weapons, were again almost entirely political in conception.

The Allied bomber offensive against Germany passed through many different phases, but it was frequently checked by the diversion of the bomber force to defensive tasks. In passing, a word about this defensive aspect. The bomber offensive was on some occasions a directly defensive measure, and, in at least one instance, the only practicable defence. The flying bomb attack was to have opened in December, 1943, with two salvoes of some sixty to seventy timed to arrive simultaneously in London late in the evening and early in the morning. Photographic reconnaissance and scientific intelligence located, interpreted, and unravelled the whole campaign before it was launched. All the launching sites so laboriously constructed were destroyed by bombing, and we got a six-months' respite while the enemy thought again. By the time he had improvised new and simpler launching sites the attack on communications had begun to disrupt his supply arrangements for bombs, fuel, and construction material, and he was never able to carry out the sustained and concentrated attacks he had planned. As regards the rocket (V2), the bomber offensive, by disrupting supply and production, was not only a very effective but the only method of limiting the scale of attack, until the land offensive, advancing under cover of complete air superiority, finally stopped all possibility of continuance of the attack by occupying the territory from which alone these weapons could be launched. As regards sea warfare, the bombing of the *Gneisenau* and *Scharnhorst* in Brest immobilised those ships, kept them off our trade routes for some nine months, and finally drove them back to German ports. Sometimes the bomber offensive was unassociated with land or sea operations, sometimes it was closely linked with them, but throughout the war it was necessarily governed by technical and tactical considerations. It is therefore rather remarkable that the final directif issued to the combined Anglo-American strategic bomber forces on 5th May, 1945, should have been identical in policy with the first directif issued to Bomber Command on 13th May, 1940, after the German invasion of the West. The directif of 1945 specified " oil and lines of communication " as the priority targets ; the directif of 1940 specified " oil installations in the Ruhr and marshalling yards " as the priority targets. To trace the changes of bombing policy round that five years' full circle would be far beyond the scope of these lectures. It would involve not only following the technical and tactical changes which marked the swaying fight for air superiority by day and night, but also analysing the inter-relationship between the bomber offensive and the Battle of Britain, the Battle of the Atlantic, the Mediterranean campaign, the war in Russia, and the final assault in North-West Europe. All I can do here is to indicate a few of the main factors which determined the changes in policy.

Target systems for air attack may be broadly divided into two classes : point targets and common denominators. Key points, or " panaceas," as they were cynically called by those who disbelieved in them, were vulnerable parts of the industrial or military structure, the destruction of which might wreck the whole ; they included such targets as aluminium plants, accumulator factories, ball-bearing plants, molybdenum mines, hydrogen peroxide plants (for " V " weapons), experimental stations, Army headquarters, and similar places which were either centres of control or bottlenecks in vital industries. The selection of key points is designed to strike at the centre. If that is impossible the tendency is to be forced to strike at the points on the periphery—the assembly plants, the depôts, the dumps, the airfields, etc. Common denominator targets I would define as railways, canals, power plants, iron and steel plants, oil ; targets which are probably dispersed geographically, but the destruction of which would collectively affect the whole war effort. This is a somewhat arbitrary division, but it does, I think, exemplify two entirely different approaches to the problem. At the same time the question immediately arises : where do the so-called " area " attacks on towns fit into this classification ? An awkward question, since they may come under either heading. When, early in 1942, Bomber Command were given the directif specifying the principal industrial cities of the Ruhr as first priority targets, the operations to be " focused on the morale of the enemy civil population and in particular of the industrial workers," this was clearly a common denominator target system—the enemy war industries were to be attacked by demoralising the workers. On the other hand, the attacks on Berlin were directed against the city as the centre of the Nazi Government and also as the centre of the radio and electrical industry—in other words, a point target. This may sound academic, but I do not think it is : the distinctions I have drawn are due to differences in object, and I am sure it is the object which is the important thing.

The difficulty about all this is that practical

technical limitations to bombing operations drastically affected the conduct of operations ; political considerations also affected them, and it is all but impossible to disentangle the strategic and economic from the political, technical, and tactical factors, all of which contributed towards the compilation of most of the bombing directifs during the war. I have already referred to the miscalculation we had made as to the ability of our bombers to operate by day without fighter escort—a miscalculation which led to our concentration on night bombing. By thus avoiding one difficulty, however, we involved ourselves in others, and during the first six months after bombing operations began there were frequent changes in the directifs given to Bomber Command.

Some of these changes were due to the rapid changes in the general war situation—during the brief campaign in France, Bomber Command were frequently diverted from the direct attack on Germany to try to assist the land forces (in accordance with our undertaking to France at the Anglo-French staff conversations in 1939) ; when invasion threatened, they were directed to attack the " invasion ports " ; oil was removed from the target list in view of the large captures of oil the enemy had made, and it was later replaced on the list ; the German air force, its industry and its airfields began to rank high on the target list ; U-boat yards and ports on the Bay of Biscay also came on to the list. These changes, most of them defensive, against submarine or surface ship attacks on our shipping, or against the air attack on U.K., were the result of various critical situations in which we found ourselves. But in the meantime practical experience more and more showed that changes of a different character were also needed. In the first place it soon became evident that the bomber force then available was quite inadequate in numbers or hitting power for the innumerable tasks it was being given. Too many targets were being attacked with too little force. In July, 1940, for example, thirty-one oil targets were attacked, twenty of them with less than twenty tons of bombs. Again, in the two summer months of 1940, a total of some 3,000 tons was dispersed on targets of oil, power, chemicals and explosives, aircraft factories and airfields, aluminium plants, docks and ports, and communications—i.e. less than half the tonnage dropped in less than an hour in front of the British Army at Caen in 1944. Similarly in 1941 a policy of attacking railways in the Ruhr and Rhineland showed disappointing results. Not only was our effort being dispersed, but also it was evident that the effect of a given tonnage of our bombs had been over-estimated. Coupled with this was a problem directly resulting from our adoption of night bombing. It soon became obvious that until our standard of navigation at night and methods of target recognition had been greatly improved, it was useless to expect our bombing, except on bright moonlight nights, to have any success against point targets. At the best, therefore, only during about a quarter of any month could precise results be expected. As early as September, 1940, as a result of the indiscriminate character of German raids on England, it was decided that our bombers, if they failed to find their primary targets, need not, as they had previously done, bring their bombs back, but were free to aim them at secondary targets—even though the latter were in built-up areas ; and later in January, 1941, after the heavy German attacks on London and other large cities in U.K., German industrial towns were specified as secondary targets —the primary targets at that time being oil targets. This and similar later modifications of the bomber policy, which ultimately had as one of its objects " morale of the German civil population and in particular of the industrial workers," gradually removed a restriction which would in itself have very greatly limited our attacks and their effect ; for had they at that time been restricted to clear moonlight nights, they could only have been very intermittent, whereas all experience went to show that it was essential for attacks to be repeated and sustained if they were to have real effect— whether material or moral. Moreover, the development of the enemy night fighter defence more and more made moonlight attacks very expensive in casualties.

The policy of " area " bombing was based on economic as well as operational considerations. From the economic point of view it was considered by our Economic Intelligence that the German economy was fully stretched, and that any general loss to German industry as a whole would have to be borne by the munitions industry. It was calculated that by attacks on the urban areas of industrial towns not only would a large proportion of the workers be rendered homeless and their morale affected, but there would also be a proportionate destruction of industrial plant, sources of power, means of transportation, public utilities, etc., and as much as a third or more of the total German output of armaments would be affected. We now know that the German economy was in fact not stretched until 1944. It is now evident that it was not until 1942 that the Nazis began to realise that they had not won the war; it was not till 1943 that they began to make a real effort to mobilise their full productive power. Till then, even munition factories had normally only been working on single shift, production of normal consumer goods had been continuing, women were not really mobilised. As a result there was reserve capacity available to replace war damage, and when Speer took control of war production he was able during 1943 and part at least of 1944, not merely to maintain, but in many cases greatly to increase production. I have already quoted the immense increase in fighter production. Similar increases were achieved in weapons, ammunition and tanks.

Our economic intelligence is now proved to have been seriously at fault. The fact, however, that Speer, in spite of the devastation of so many industrial towns, was able by various far-reaching measures to increase war production does not by any means imply that these attacks failed to affect the German war effort. It is, for example, notable that despite all these measures, involving as they did drastic limitation to the types of armament, lowering of standards of materials, use of slave labour, etc., the increase in production was checked by the air offensive during the second half of 1943, before it made its final spurt to its peak in July, 1944, and subsequent collapse. In 1943 a force of over 600,000 and in 1944 nearly 900,000 was maintained in Germany to man the A.A. defences —not far short of the peak total strength of the R.A.F. all over the world. Even in 1942 the figure was 439,000. A.A. guns took between 25 per cent. and 30 per cent. of the value of Germany's total weapon production. Perhaps the clearest indication that the attacks were hurting is given by the growth of the German night fighter force from virtually nothing to 150 in November, 1940 ; 250 by July, 1942 ; 550 by July, 1943 ; 800 by Spring, 1944 ; and 1,250 by the end of 1944. Let us also remember that the weight of attack in 1943 was only one-fifth of what it reached in 1944. I have referred to the battle for air superiority, to the German loss of the initiative : a vital phase of that battle was fought out in the night skies " over his vital living space."

It was a hard-fought battle and new and ever-changing tactics and technique had to be hammered out by hard-won experience. I doubt whether it is fully realised that in war every single bombing operation is merely one item in a complex campaign, and, to be successful, has to fit in to a general plan of operations which may cover the whole theatre of war and extend over a period of days, weeks, or even months. Weather, phases of the moon, length of darkness, enemy fighter strength and tactics, enemy defence organisation for guns, lights, radar, and fighter control ; ever-changing technique of navigation, target marking, and bombing—all these factors, and more, affect the selection and the type and location of targets. To develop the equipment and technique, and to train the air-crews to attain a high degree of pin-point accuracy in the face of enemy opposition and under every-day weather conditions, was a long-drawn-out struggle fought at a heavy cost, and it was not until 1944 that it was possible to deliver a heavy attack in Germany with real precision. When, however, that stage was reached it was possible to place a heavier concentration on a precise target by non-visual than by visual methods. The effectiveness of our night attacks was then assured.

The American Air Force, which began to operate in Europe in late 1942, also had to pass through a similar hard school in developing their day attacks. Like Bomber Command, they found that penetration over Germany without fighter cover was prohibitive in cost. On 17th August, 1943, two attacks, on ball-bearing factories at Schweinfurt and the Messerschmitt plant at Regensburg, cost them 15·7 per cent. and 16·4 per cent. casualties respectively. Even later still, in October, 1943, they sustained a higher overall percentage of losses than in any previous month; one particular raid on Schweinfurt on 14th October (when the penetration escort could get no further than Aachen, and the withdrawal escort failed to appear owing to bad weather over England) resulted in the loss of 20·6 per cent. of the aircraft despatched. Gradually they were able to equip their force with escort fighters which, ultimately in 1944, were able to provide cover as far as Berlin. They also had tactical and technical problems to solve in order to achieve concentration and accuracy under every-day weather conditions.

Since early 1943 the British and the expanding U.S. Bomber forces had operated on a common directif issued by the Combined Chiefs of Staff. The severe fighting for air superiority, both by day and night, coupled with the paramount need for a very high degree of air superiority for the assault on Europe which was looming nearer, had led to the German Air Force, and especially the fighter force, being specified as the primary target system : the U.S. force to attack key factories and associated industries by day, and Bomber Command to carry out area attacks by night on towns specially associated with aircraft production. During six days of exceptionally fair weather in February, 1944, the U.S. Air Forces (from U.K. and Italian bases) carried out an accurate and highly successful series of attacks on the main German fighter plants. The scale of attacks was maintained till August, 1944, but after the February attacks the aircraft industry was put under the control of Speer. In a previous lecture I referred to the apparent anomaly of increased production despite successful attack. The fact was that in the aircraft industry, as in other parts of German armament industry, there was spare capacity and there were supplies of slave labour who were not allowed the luxury of " morale "—nearly 50 per cent. of the labour force in the German aircraft industry in 1944 was composed of foreign workers and prisoners of war. Also Speer was evidently a man of outstanding ability and drive. Nevertheless, though the industry was producing the numbers on the ground, the Luftwaffe were losing the battle in the air.

It has been calculated that during 1943 the bomber offensive cost the German some 10 per cent. of his total production and less than 5 per cent. of his war production. Up to this stage, therefore, judged purely by war production figures, it would appear that the attacks on neither of the two main target systems—the industrial towns and the German aircraft industry—had achieved their primary object of " the progressive destruction and dislocation of the German military, industrial, and economic system, and the undermining of the morale of the German people to a point where their capacity for armed resistance is fatally weakened." This is, however, by no means the whole story. In the first place we must remember that the total weight of attack during the first four years the war was considerably less than that dropped in the five months in 1945. Next, and of paramount importance, were the firm foundations to air superiority which were laid during this phase— the vital factor affecting the whole latter course of the war. The air war was being fought out over Germany and not over Britain. Then there was the question of German productive capacity : we have seen that for more than three years of the war Germany was not fully stretched; she had capacity employed on non-essential production which served as a cushion to absorb the shock of the injuries to her war production : it is clear that the first phases of the bomber offensive, by forcing wholesale transfer and dispersal of war industry, punctured that cushion and rendered the German war economy specially vulnerable to the later attack on communications and oil.

Early in 1944 the projected land assault on Europe began to take absolute priority over all other military operations. The days when air power afforded the only means of attacking Germany were passing. The question now was how could air power be best exercised to assist the assault? The prime requirement, of course, was air superiority. I have already discussed that. It remained a continuing commitment. Apart from that, and from purely tactical short-term support (the "softening" operations), were two main target systems selected—oil and communications. The immediate problem facing the invasion of Normandy, after the initial lodgment had been secured, was to build up the Allied forces in Normandy as quickly as, or quicker than, the enemy could collect his reinforcements : our forces and all their stores and equipment had to come by sea and be landed across beaches, whereas the enemy had one of the best rail and road systems in Europe at his disposal. It was considered that, since the enemy would almost certainly be holding ample stocks of oil in France to meet the immediate emergency, attack on the oil industry was not likely to give the immediate assistance which the assault required. It was therefore decided that the primary target system for the Allied strategic bomber forces should be the transportation system upon which the movements of the enemy reinforcements would depend.

At the end of 1943 there was completed a very detailed analysis of the effects of the air attacks on the communications in Sicily and Southern Italy. That analyis indicated that a series of attacks on a very limited number of main railway centres had practically paralysed the rail system throughout Sicily and Southern Italy. *Diagram No.* 6 gives an idea of the early stage in the process —incidentally it shows up some of the " unseen " war that went on behind the battle scenes of North Africa. The railway systems which would feed the Normandy battlefields were far more dense and extensive than those in Italy, but after careful examination it was decided that the same principles would apply as regards vulnerability to air attack.

The plan called for attacks on seventy-nine rail

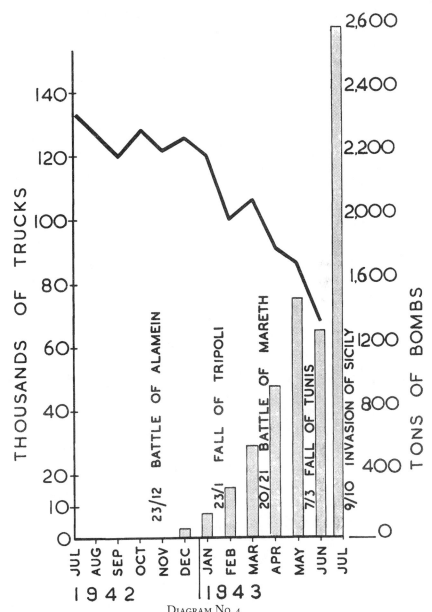

DIAGRAM No. 4

MONTHLY TOTALS OF RAILWAY TRAFFIC AT, AND BOMB
TONNAGES DROPPED ON, PRINCIPAL PORTS OF LOADING
IN SICILY.

centres in Northern France and Belgium and fourteen in South-Eastern France, the latter to be carried out by U.S. air forces based in Italy. The attacks began on March 6th and were completed shortly before D Day. Of the total of some 67,000 tons, 45,000 were dropped by Bomber Command in a series of highly concentrated and extremely accurate attacks. Concentrated precision attacks at night were now tactically and technically possible. The primary object of these attacks was the destruction of locomotive sheds and of maintenance and repair facilities, but it was calculated that in addition they would dislocate the marshalling yards, through lines, signalling equipment, and destroy or damage locomotives and rolling stock. About the middle of March a precipitous fall began in the volume of traffic. In the Region Nord which had received the heaviest share of the attacks, traffic was down to 20 per cent. of its pre-attack level, and by D Day it was down to 13 per cent. Moreover, the effects of this dislocation spread far and wide. By the end of May, traffic entering the Nord from outside France was barely 20 per cent. of its February level. In France as a whole, traffic was down to 50 per cent. in May, and by D Day 30 per cent. of its normal volume (see Diagram No. 5). German troop movements were naturally the last to suffer —economic and non-military traffic was sacrificed first. But troop movements themselves were utterly disorganised. I only quote one example of two Panzer divisions rushed across from Poland during

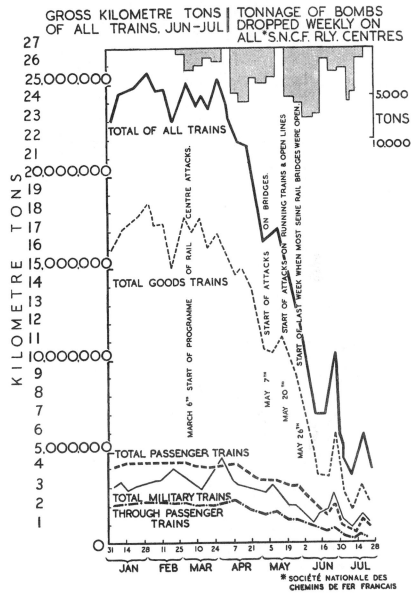

GROSS KILOMETRE TONS | TONNAGE OF BOMBS
OF ALL TRAINS, JUN-JUL | DROPPED WEEKLY ON
ALL *S.N.C.F. RLY. CENTRES

27
26
25,000,000
24
23
22
21
20,000,000
19
18
17
16
15,000,000
14
13
12
11
10,000,000
9
8
7
6
5,000,000
4
3
2
1
O

KILOMETRE TONS

5,000
TONS
10,000

TOTAL OF ALL TRAINS

TOTAL GOODS TRAINS

CENTRE ATTACKS.

MARCH 6TH START OF PROGRAMME

START OF ATTACKS ON BRIDGES.

START OF ATTACKS ON RUNNING TRAINS & OPEN LINES

START OF LAST WEEK WHEN MOST SEINE RAIL BRIDGES WERE OPEN.

MAY 7TH

MAY 20TH

MAY 26TH

TOTAL PASSENGER TRAINS

TOTAL MILITARY TRAINS
THROUGH PASSENGER
TRAINS

31 14 28 | 11 25 | 10 24 | 7 21 | 5 19 | 2 16 30 | 14 28
JAN | FEB | MAR | APR | MAY | JUN | JUL

* SOCIÉTÉ NATIONALE DES
CHEMINS DE FER FRANÇAIS

DIAGRAM No. 5

VOLUME OF RAILWAY TRAFFIC IN FRANCE—1944.

the first week of the landings. They travelled the
1,000 miles to France in five days, but had to
detrain at points as far east as Nancy, for only the
armour could be sent on by train, and that with
difficulty, and the remainder of their journey took
nine days. In other cases journeys scheduled to
take five days took fifteen days, and even so became
chaotic. Units arrived in the battle zone in small
parties without essential equipment and were committed piecemeal to battle.

These attacks began three months before the
actual landings in Normandy : they had achieved
their object in two and a half months and had
virtually paralysed the railway system in France
and Belgium. They were, however, only a part,
though it is now clear that they were the decisive
part, of a wide pattern of operations by which
Allied air power was exercised to help the Allied
armies establish themselves on the continent of
Europe. During the last fortnight before the
assault, bombers of the tactical air forces, who
had already contributed some effort towards the
railway attacks, turned their attention to the railway bridges, and once the assault had begun
fighter bombers harried every road and railway
along which German reinforcements or supplies
were moving. The Germans had ample stocks of
fuel and ammunition in France, but the fighting
troops went short because transport by road or
rail became utterly disorganised ; formations and
units arrived late and in disorganised fragments
lacking essential equipment ; communications of

all kinds broke down. Finally, before any major Allied advance, the Germans facing the advance were smothered in a sudden deluge of high explosive from the air—as much as 7,000 tons of bombs in half an hour. In May, 1943, the Italian island fortress of Pantelleria had been the subject of a full-scale experiment in the exercise of air power, and brought to surrender by a systematic and concentrated air attack. In June, 1944, the objective was the Fortress of Europe, and the garrison was German ; there was hard fighting to be done, but the lessons learnt in the Mediterranean laboratory were applied and proved their worth. As von Rundstedt put it, it was " all a question of air force, air force and again air force " ; or more calmly : " The main difficulties which arose for us at the time of the invasion were the systematic preparations by your air force ; the smashing of the main lines of communications, particularly the railway junctions. We had prepared for various eventualities . . . that all came to nothing or was rendered impossible by the destruction of railway communications, railway stations, etc. The second thing was the attack on the roads, on marching columns, etc., so that it was impossible to move anyone at all by day, whether a column or an individual, that is to say carry fuel or ammunition. That also meant that the bringing up of the armoured divisions was also out of the question, quite impossible. And the third thing was this carpet bombing . . . Those were the main things which caused the general collapse."

The pendulum had indeed swung over since the Wehrmacht had swept across France four years earlier.

The attack of the strategic air forces on the railway arteries of France and Belgium had, however, had results wider and deeper than merely disorganising the German reply to our landings. When Brussels was occupied we were fortunate enough to secure a mass of records of railway movements kept by the methodical German, and amongst them a chart analysing the flow of rail traffic in the area covering North-East France and Belgium. It confirms in a most unmistakable manner what had been hinted at by the experience in the Mediterranean. Firstly, it confirms that the attack on the rail centres did in fact paralyse the whole rail system. But it also shows that this paralysis was contagious and that it had devastating economic effects. Military traffic had been maintained (though we have already seen how utterly disorganised even that residual traffic was)—but only maintained at the expense of practically all other traffic. The iron ore traffic to the Saar, which was a highly important element in the Rhineland steel industry, was stopped. The coke traffic was stopped. The coal traffic was stopped—I think the effect of that needs no comment!

These facts had an obvious bearing on future

policy as regards Germany itself. It was clear
that no country in the grip of such a paralysis of
her communications could maintain war production, maintain forces in the field, or even continue to function as an organised economic state.
Moreover, it was a paralysis which had set in with
surprising rapidity at the cost of a relatively modest
bombing effort, and consequently with relatively
little actual destruction. The question was whether
Germany, with her denser and more extended rail
system, was equally susceptible.

There was, however, one other main element
in the German economy to be considered. You
will remember the first directif of Bomber Command in 1940—" rail communications and oil."
The German oil situation had been kept under
very careful and thorough observation throughout.
Germany had always been very near the safety
margin as regards oil fuel, especially aviation
gasoline. Captured stocks in the early stages of
the war had helped materially, but heavy demands
for the Russian and Mediterranean campaigns had
swallowed up stocks in 1941 and 1942. In 1943
the long-range plan for provision of a series of
synthetic oil plants began to pay dividends, and
early in 1944 the stock situation was improving
as the output of these plants increased. But the
whole position depended on these plants ; and
now that an Allied strategic bomber force was
established in Italy, all the plants in Germany,
Austria, Hungary and Roumania on which Germany depended were within striking range of

Allied air forces, either from the north or the south. Early in May, the attack on transportation having developed so effectively, a proportion of the available effort was switched to the oil targets. First the main effort came from the XVth U.S. Air Force in Italy against plants in Roumania, Hungary, Austria, Czechoslovakia, Poland and Silesia—the attacks included the mining of the Danube by a force of R.A.F. bombers which practically closed the upper Danube and sank twenty-nine tankers, thereby helping to make the offensive against railways in South-East Europe even more effective. By the end of September, when control of the strategic air forces, which since March had been in the hands of S.C.A.E.F., reverted to the C.A.S. and the C.G. of the U.S.A.A.F., over 200 attacks had been made and over 60,000 tons had been dropped on oil targets in Greater Germany—where the effects of our attacks were incidentally still further aggravated by the over-running of the Roumanian supply sources by the Russians in August. A few days later, in a new directif, oil targets were put as first priority. The campaign against oil continued till early April, 1945. Between October and December bad weather somewhat reduced the effectiveness of the attack, and in late December and early January attacks on oil had to be relaxed in order to concentrate against von Rundstedt's communications during the Ardennes battle. It is now evident, however, that vital damage had been done as early as June. On May 30th Speer had reported to Hitler that " with the attacks on the hydrogenation plants, systematic bombing raids on economic targets have started at the most dangerous point. The only hope is that the enemy, too, has got an air staff. Only if it had as little comprehension of economic targets as ours would there be some hope that after a few attacks on this decisive economic target it would turn its attentions elsewhere." Fortunately, it did not turn its attention away. The Allied air forces were strong enough to deal with the day-to-day emergencies at that time without relaxing on their main tasks—transportation and oil. A month later Speer, in an urgent personal letter to Hitler, reported loss of aviation fuel up to 90 per cent. and emphasised the need for rapid repair and increased protection, " Otherwise," he said, " it will be absolutely impossible to cover the most urgent of the necessary supplies for the Wehrmacht by September ; in other words, from that time onwards there will be an unbridgeable gap which must lead to tragic results." It did.

I need not here follow the progress of the campaign and its effects : the repeated photographic reconnaissance and skilled interpretation which kept a finger on the weakening pulse and made it possible to repeat attacks just when repairs were being completed ; the repercussions of these attacks on the whole chemical industry (powder and explosives, synthetic rubber, plastics, nitrogen for agriculture, the special fuel for the rockets—all badly hit) which yielded rather unexpected additional dividends ; the repercussions of fuel shortage

on the Luftwaffe which I have already referred to ;
the repercussions on the Wehrmacht which are
more difficult to assess since here the paralysis of
communications was also a vital factor. During
the slight recovery in the fuel situation between
October and December by means of rigid and
ruthless economies, some stocks had been collected
for the Ardennes offensive. But during that period
the communications in and round the Ruhr had
been heavily attacked—the process which had been
used effectively in France and Belgium was now
being applied to the Reich itself. In mid-October,
Speer said he had reported to Hitler " about the
severe crisis obtaining in the communication system
of Western and Southern Germany owing to air
attacks," and early in November he reported :
" The planned attacks on the installations of the
Reichsbahn are of decisive significance . . . successful continuation of these attacks would be
capable of resulting in a production catastrophe of
decisive significance for the further conduct of the
war."

The true pattern of the Allied air offensive was
now becoming visible. Oil and communications
were not alternative target systems ; they were
complementary, and together they were the one
common denominator of Germany's war effort—
from the political control at the top down to the
supply of the troops in the front line. More and
more, as the Luftwaffe faded out, the Allied air
forces, strategic and tactical, concentrated against
the dual target system—rail centres (especially

those feeding the Ruhr), a few key viaducts, rail bridges, trains, key points on the main canals, oil plants, all were increasingly attacked by day and by night by the appropriate types of aircraft and weapon. And the paralysis spread. Coal piled up at the pits could not be distributed and industries all over the Reich began to close down ; shipping began to stagnate, electricity plants and gas plants began to close down. As Speer reported to Hitler in December : " The enemy has recognised that systematic attacks on our communications may have a most decisive effect in all spheres on our conduct of the war," and to his own staff that month : " Our troubles for the month to come are dictated by the communications situation which in recent months has deteriorated to a quite exceptional extent. . . . In armaments we were lucky enough to have had plenty of time. . . . In the case of communications the circumstances were different. There, these large-scale attacks were more or less started at a day's notice. . . . It is necessary to be clear in one's mind that the men who worked out the enemy's economic attack plans understood something about German economic life and that . . . there is a far-reaching and clever planning at work. We were fortunate that the enemy did not put this far-reaching plan into effect until about six or nine months ago."

On 15th March, 1945, Speer reported to Hitler, giving the figures of coal deliveries from the Ruhr, and said : " These figures mean that neither the coal supplies for shipping, for the Reichsbahn, for the gas and electricity plants, for the food economy, nor for the armament economy (which occupies the last place) can by any means be assured . . . The final collapse of the German economy can therefore be counted on with certainty within four to eight weeks. . . . After this collapse even military continuation of the war will become impossible."

Detailed analysis of German records indicates that during the first quarter of 1945 German armament production (excluding the oil industry) was down by 45 per cent. ; but that was output. Since car loadings were down to 15 per cent. and coal deliveries down to 4 per cent. of normal towards the end of March, it is clear that production itself must rapidly come to a complete standstill (*see Diagram No. 6*). Moreover, one must remember that the losses on the civilian sector of the German economy were almost certainly one and a half times to twice as great as those on the armament sector. Here was economic warfare driven home to the point of economic collapse, and with it political and military collapse. This was the unseen war.

I do not want you to think that I am suggesting that this utterly decisive result was achieved entirely by air power. It was the capture of airfields in Italy that brought the oil plants in Hungary, Austria, Roumania, etc., within effective range of the Mediterranean air forces. The freeing of France and Belgium, by enabling us to advance our navigation aids on the ground, made

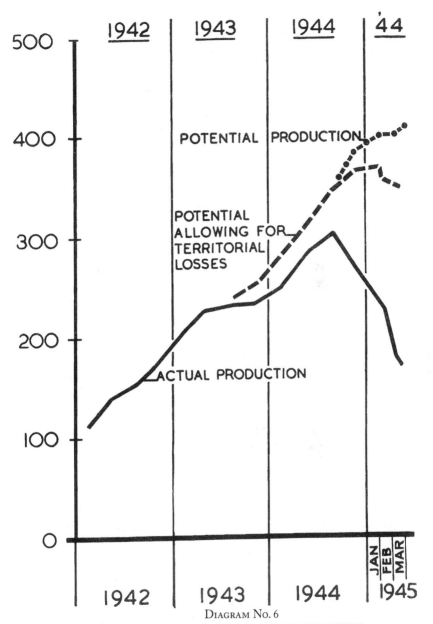

DIAGRAM No. 6

INDEX OF GERMAN ARMAMENT PRODUCTION.

(Shown as percentages of Jan–Feb., 1942 production.)

possible a greater degree of accuracy in attacks deep in Germany, and by depriving the enemy of warning and defence in depth helped the Allied air forces to obtain a higher degree of air superiority. Loss of occupied and other territories to the Allies in the West and in the East itself involved a loss to Germany of her armament production which has been calculated as being as much as 13 per cent. in the first quarter of 1945. But one can sympathise with von Rundstedt in his summing up on the failure of the Ardennes offensive : " The root of the whole trouble was air power, air power."

In my first lecture I uttered a word of warning against drawing too many conclusions from the days of military plenty towards the end of the war You may feel that I am falling into precisely that error in emphasising the decisive results achieved by the Allied air forces when they had been built up to the great strength they attained in 1944. If you feel that, I must remind you that, as well as emphasising the successes which strength made possible, I also pointed out some of the early failures due to weakness. Before the war we had tried to be strong everywhere, and only succeeded in being weak everywhere ; on land, at sea, and in the air. Fortunately, thanks in no small measure to the Germans not understanding air power, we were just strong enough in the air to hold the fort for those first three and a half years, to push the enemy air force back, and to keep it back, from the heart of our war effort. By fighting back, our air force gave us that most precious thing—time.

But three and a half years of fighting—fighting, not to win the war—that came later—but to avoid losing it. We started by fighting in the last ditch, and it was four years before the land, sea and air Goliath we were building was ready to begin to fight to win. On neither military nor economic grounds can we afford to risk a repetition of that. We must re-assess the problem of our security and re-allocate our defence effort so as to ensure the maximum power with the minimum of expenditure of man-power and material. During these lectures I have posed a number of questions which bear on this problem. I do not propose to attempt here to answer them. What I have tried to do is to set out as objectively and factually as possible some of the effects of the impact of air power on the course of World War II.

But here, for what they are worth, are my own beliefs based on what I have seen and learnt during the war. I am utterly convinced that the outstanding and vital lesson of this last war is that air power is the dominant factor in this modern world and that, though the methods of exercising it will change, it will remain the dominant factor so long as power determines the fate of nations. I believe that sea power is still vital to our very existence, and I am sure that sea power, properly exercised, can still be one of the keys to our security and not merely a commitment. I also believe that, in view of the inevitable dominance of air power, purely passive defence would be certain and painful suicide ; it is peace with teeth, and the teeth must be able to bite hard and swiftly. In 1941 General Smuts spoke of air power as " the Air, the architect of Victory " ; properly understood and used, I believe it can be the guardian of peace until that happy day when nations realise finally that wars don't pay.

AIR, LAND AND SEA WARFARE

Sir Arthur Tedder on the Strategic Lessons of the World War

General Sir Hastings Ismay, K.C.B., D.S.O., took the chair at the Royal United Service Institution on January 9 when Marshal of the Royal Air Force Sir Arthur Tedder, G.C.B., (soon to be known by a still more august title) delivered a lecture on "Air, Land and Sea Warfare." General Ismay, with his experience as Chief of Staff to the Minister of Defence, was a very suitable chairman for a lecture, which laid heavy stress on the need for all three Services to work together.

Sir Arthur began by explaining that he had not written his lecture as Chief of the Air Staff, but as the recent Deputy Supreme Commander under General Eisenhower, and the views[he would express were his personal opinions. He mentioned that after the San Francisco Conference Field Marshal Smuts had described the peace at which all were aiming as "Peace with Teeth." Sir Arthur said that the teeth must be sound. We must analyse the lessons of the late war, and dig out the underlying truth. We must ask ourselves whether our national war effort had been employed in the most economical way, and also ask why the Germans lost the war. By economy he meant efficiency, not doing things on the cheap. A nation at war was like a boxer, who must have the right muscles developed so that he gets each punch home with the maximum effect and the minimum effort. In the first great war we had started with a slogan of "Business as usual," but we found it did not pay, and gave it up. In the recent war Germany tried to maintain "Business as usual" in some respects up to 1944.

AFTERWORD

FIVE SEPARATE WARS

Sir Arthur said that there was one war of production, fought in the factories; another of civil defence; another on the sea; another on land; and another in the air. Each of these had its own unity. He explained that all these combined to create one unity of national effort.

He was still of the opinion that there was such a thing as air warfare as apart from sea warfare and land warfare, but he did not fully develop that thesis. He said that the Germans never got their land and sea forces closely knit. They used to boast about their *Luftwaffe,* but they never looked on it as anything but an ancillary to their army. In the early days the *Luftwaffe* could intervene in a land battle without first having to win the air battle. At the end the *Luftwaffe* showed up as not having been properly trained or equipped.

It might be necessary at the beginning of a campaign for all sides of an Air Force to work together to gain air superiority. He asked his audience to contrast the early days when the British sea convoys had to sneak along the coast with the final days when the seas round Britain were thronged with craft of all sorts in great numbers. That was because we had gained air superiority.

Sir Arthur said that he considered the outstanding features of air power were flexibility and the power of concentrating. Air power in penny packets was worse than useless. But air unity was not exclusive; operations in the three elements were interdependent.

OLD AND NEW STANDARDS

To illustrate his point he recounted the campaign of Crete. After our defeat in Greece Crete lay in a semi-circle of enemy airfields. Our few airfields (both in Greece and in Crete) had no possibility of dispersal, owing to lack of engineers, and no defence, owing to lack of guns. By the old standards we held command of the seas; but 80 per cent of the reinforcements and supplies from Egypt had to turn back; 10 per cent were sunk, and only 10 per cent got through. That was because we did not command the air. So we learnt our lesson; we must have air superiority in quantity as well as in quality. We must be frank, said Sir Arthur repeatedly. It was no use having a good fleet or a good army without air power. Gradually the need of a balance of forces was realised. Then the land war in the Mediterranean became a battle for airfields and we won it.

Only with mutual faith and knowledge could you get the three unities working as one. It was essential that all commanders should know what the other two Services were doing. In the air we constantly had to choose between a faggot, which was hard to break, and a number of single sticks, each of which was weak. We stuck to the faggots. Mutual faith and understanding brought one to personalities. One must have men who will fit together. We owed more than we could realise to General Eisenhower. To achieve mutual faith one must be ruthless; give men a little time to get to work together, but if some individuals could not do it, they must be got rid of.

Sir Arthur turned back to the question of mistakes. He pointed out that in 1940 the Germans could not stop the evacuation from Dunkirk or face an invasion of England, though the land defenders were mostly armed with shot-guns and pikes; while in 1943 there was no German "Dunkirk" from Tunisia, and in 1944 the Germans, despite years of preparation, could not stop the Allies from invading the Continent.

Now we had to face the future. In his opinion, said Sir Arthur, the key words for the future were flexibility and speed. The future lay, not with a slow-growing Goliath, but with David.